James Jenkins

November, 1998

Rindge, N.H.

*Amos Fortune*
FREE MAN

*Books for Young People by Elizabeth Yates*

WITH PIPE, PADDLE, AND SONG

AN EASTER STORY

CAROLINA'S COURAGE

SOMEDAY YOU'LL WRITE

AMOS FORTUNE, FREE MAN

PRUDENCE CRANDALL, WOMAN OF COURAGE

PEBBLE IN A POOL,
THE WIDENING CIRCLES OF DOROTHY CANFIELD FISHER'S LIFE

PATTERNS ON THE WALL

RAINBOW ROUND THE WORLD: THE STORY OF UNICEF

MOUNTAIN BORN

A PLACE FOR PETER

CHILDREN OF THE BIBLE

YOUR PRAYERS AND MINE

# *Amos Fortune*
# FREE MAN

## ELIZABETH YATES

*Illustrated by Nora S. Unwin*

DUTTON CHILDREN'S BOOK  NEW YORK

ISBN 0-525-25570-2

Published in the United States by
Dutton Children's Books,
a division of Penguin Books USA Inc.
375 Hudson Street, New York, New York 10014

Gift 8/04

50 49 48 47 46 45

CURR
E
185.97
.F73
.Y3
1963

*For* **N. S. U.**
*dear partner in many books*
*and good friend through the years*

# ACKNOWLEDGMENTS

MY THANKS ARE DUE to the following for the help given me while writing this book: to Mrs. Mildred Peterson McKay, State Librarian, Concord, New Hampshire, for her interest, for her tireless tracking down in various library files actual material on Amos Fortune, and for the books she supplied me with which gave me much necessary background; to F. Alexander Magoun, chairman of the Amos Fortune Committee and neighbor in Jaffrey, for his kindness in reading the manuscript, and for his keen criticism and many wise suggestions; to Mrs. Evelyn Ruffle, librarian, East Jaffrey, New Hampshire, for her unremitting and finally fruitful search after the original Amos Fortune papers which had apparently disappeared, but which are now available in the library at East Jaffrey for all to see. And, not least, are thanks due to my husband, William McGreal, for the confidence he gives me when I assign to myself what seems to be an almost impossible task.

# CONTENTS

*Amos Fortune*
FREE MAN

# AFRICA 1725

⊂⊃ NIGHT CAME DOWN SWIFTLY over the equatorial forest. There was no lingering of daylight; but, after the snuffing out of the sun, darkness and the bright appearing of stars. No silence came with the darkness, for this was a night alive with song and movement. In the village of the At-mun-shi the people were gathering for their mystic dance that would welcome in the time of herbage, the time for the planting of corn.

3

Into the center of the clearing surrounded by small conical huts that was the village, a wooden drum had been brought. With solemn reverence Saala, the old wise man of the tribe, approached and began beating it. It was not long the only sound in the darkness. Soon smaller drums in distant parts of the clearing took up a beating. Then wooden flutes joined in from the outskirts of the village. Their sound was muted at first but it grew sharper and higher as the men blowing the flutes came nearer. Joined by the beaters on the drums, the sound quickened in pace and fervor as all gathered in a group around the great drum, coming into time with Saala's rhythmic beating. The moon rose high enough for the light to filter through the heavy foliage. It gleamed on the black bodies of the men, on the faces of the women and children who had been gathering in the clearing, summoned by the music and swaying with it like a field of tall grass before the wind.

When the flutes and the drums ceased, all the At-mun-shi turned and faced the same way, making obeisance to their chief who sat on a raised platform at one end of the clearing, the moon full on him and his children standing beside him. At-mun, the young prince, was tall and powerfully built, though he had seen no more than fifteen summers. He carried his head high and his eyes flashed. Ath-mun, the twelve year old princess, smiled shyly at her tribespeople, then turned to whisper in her father's ear. She leaned against him, hoping to hide the deformed leg that—but for her father's love— would have caused her to have been drowned as an infant. Only the sacrifice of the imperfect to the God of Life could assure protection for the perfect. But the chief had gone against his tribal code and sacrificed his favorite dog to keep his infant daughter and thus far the God of Life had wreaked no vengeance on him. The At-mun-shi were as pagan as all the tribes in Africa, but they were peaceable and they were, as well, intense in their love of freedom.

The chief acknowledged the obeisance of his people and spread his hands before them, palms down, indicating that they might do their own pleasure for the next space of time. The people stood quietly while more and more of the At-mun-shi came in from the jungle to join the group in the clearing. At the outskirts of the village, beyond the circle of conical huts, they laid down their knives and spears. The weapons, lying in their piles without men to hold them, gave back the moonlight's sheen in harmless splendor. This was a night of peace and during it no At-mun-shi would bear anything symbolic of killing. This was the time when the earth was reborn.

Saala commenced beating the great drum again and all the smaller drums followed, but in such unison that it was like single reverberations on the night; then flutes picked up the sound. The dancers gathered themselves together, twelve men well matched in size. Slowly they made their way around the open space in the clearing, shoulders, hips, feet translating the sound of flutes and drums into movement. The music quickened, steps grew longer, and guttural voices uttered the incantation which had been said by their fathers and would be said by their children:

Earth our mother, Sun our father,
Watch while we plant.
Moon our sister, Rain our brother,
Aid the seeds to bear fruit
That the harvest may be good,
Enough for us and our children.

Over and over the words were repeated as family after family of the At-mun-shi joined in until the forest beyond the clearing echoed and re-echoed the chant. Then, at a signal from the chief, the chanting ceased and the dancers fell back, leaving an open space in their midst.

At-mun bowed to his father and with a series of leaps covered the distance from the raised platform at one end of the clearing to the open space. There he stood in his full height, lifting his hands palms up to the sky. Then swiftly he knelt, palms down to the earth, bowing his head and pressing his lips to the soil: all that he had, all that he ever would be, he gave to his people. He was their prince, someday to be their chief. He could not do otherwise. Rising, he bounded back to the platform and knelt before his sister. Taking her in his arms, frail and slight of body as she was, he danced with her before the people.

"He is strong," they said to each other, voices hushed like the wind through the bamboo.

"He is beautiful," they said, smiling to each other like the first light of dawn.

"When the time comes he will rule us well," said Saala who had seen many rulers.

An old woman tapped her head, "Not with this will he rule," she said, "but so," and she laid her hand upon her heart. "See how he is with his sister."

At-mun danced on, swirling his light burden above the heads of the people, then swinging her low. Always Ath-mun smiled, for with her brother she felt safe. At-mun's expression never changed until the dance was over, then he set the small dark girl down on the platform and stood before his father, head bowed. The chief laid his hand on his son's head in approval. At-mun swung around and faced his people while the smile that flashed from his face might have dazzled the moon itself.

The drums and the flutes began again to build up an air, and the people began again to sway in time with it. At-mun, young, strong, tireless, leapt into their midst, leading the At-mun-shi in a tribal dance until the whole clearing seethed with joyous ecstatic motion. Dawn was still far distant and this was the night of the year when no one would sleep.

Dawn was further off than the invaders creeping silently through the jungle, a hundred black men commanded by three whites. Stealthily they surrounded the village, making sure that their line was within the piles of knives and spears that the At-mun-shi had left. Dropping to their knees at a given signal, they held their guns, took aim and waited, tense and silent, for another signal. One of the white men raised his arm and a hundred muskets blazed into the night. The dancing people stopped and looked skyward. Then they fell to their knees, bewildered, fearful only of one thing that they had offended the Spirit of the Night. The chief slumped forward. All of the muskets but one had been aimed into the treetops.

At-mun rose to his feet and bounded across the clearing to kneel by his father. Then, in the strange and fearful stillness of the jungle night, he knew what had happened. He stood tall and held out his hands to his people, but no smile flashed from his lips.

There was not time for the At-mun-shi to acknowledge the gesture of their new chief. With cries and shouts, the slavers advanced on the village. Seeing them, the At-mun-shi screamed wildly and ran across the clearing, trying to reach their chief who stood above them in strength and power, symbolizing protection. But the slavers, advancing among them, tossed the At-mun-shi about like leaves in a wind. Seizing the strongest and tallest, they quickly clamped wrist and ankle shackles on them, thrusting aside the old men and women, the little children.

A white man approached the platform where At-mun was standing, his arm around Ath-mun. The white man uttered a volley of words, sharp as the sound of the muskets had been in At-mun's ears and less meaningful. But At-mun would not lower himself to respond. When the slaver advanced and tried to separate the brother and sister, At-mun's hold only tightened on the girl. The white man hesitated; he had seen fire flashing from the eyes of the tall black youth and he was afraid. A second white man, fully armed, approached from one side and seeing him gave the slaver courage. Stepping forward, he seized Ath-mun and hurled her to the ground. When At-mun reached out to help her the two whites secured his wrists with bamboo withes and threw him down to chain his ankles.

"He's a likely one," the slaver muttered, "and should fetch a good price, but he's dangerous. Tighten those irons."

Dawn came. The At-mun-shi men and some of their women stood in a long line chained together in the clearing surrounded by the conical huts. Those whom the slavers had not wanted cowered together, too stunned for any utterance. Commands were barked out that meant nothing to the At-mun-shi. Then the crack of a lash started the long line moving slowly. Seeing them disappear into the jungle, the old men and women and the little children set up a low wailing. It was so soft at first that it was scarcely audible, but it grew in volume and intensity. Desolate, deprived of their youth, their strength, their leadership,what were a handful of old people and children to do in the jungle?

The line filed slowly on as the best of the At-mun-shi with bowed heads and bowed shoulders stumbled into the unknown. Only a youth at the end of the line still carried his head high. Past the raised platform they went, past the huddled form of a young girl, and only the sound of her weeping let them know that she was alive. Passing her, At-mun suddenly bent low and said something to her, then he raised his head again. The slaver, bringing up the rear, came forward with his lash. At-mun cringed as he felt it, but he uttered no sound, though for the rest of his life his back would bear the marks made on it by the white man's lash.

Ath-mun lifted her head and listened until she could no longer hear the dull thud of footsteps echoing on the jungle floor. She rose to her feet with difficulty, then holding her hands open and outspread as was the custom of her tribe she advanced slowly toward her people. At-mun had reminded her that her birth had made her the servant of her people. He was still a prince, though chains bound him, and she was a princess. Neither one could escape the work they had been born to do.

# THE MIDDLE PASSAGE

⊂⊋ THE CAPTIVES WERE LED through the jungle from early dawn until noon, when they reached the bank of a wide river. There they were given water but no food. Under the watchful eyes and ever-pointed muskets of their captors, they were allowed a brief rest while canoes were readied for the journey down stream. Coarse shouts and loud-voiced commands in a meaningless tongue filled the air. The At-mun-shi people, now so tired and hungry that their fright and bewilderment were secondary, squatted on the ground with heads between their knees. At-mun looked from one to another of them, signalling with his eyes, and through the weary group a quiver of hope ran uniting them to him. Whatever they had left behind, whatever lay ahead, their chief was with them, their traditional father. They knew that he would care for them.

At-mun realized that he and his people were being enslaved by power and cunning and that they must bide their time until they could effect their release in some way. Slavery was a phase of tribal war, as old as African life itself, but the At-mun-shi had always been a free people, putting no bonds on others and resisting any put on them. At-mun looked from one face to another. He was troubled in his heart about his people for something had made them abashed and spiritless.

The slavers ate well and drank freely. Then, while the sun was at its highest, pouring fierce heat upon the land, they crept under crudely constructed shelters of wide palm leaves and slept. No one took any thought of the At-mun-shi.

Under the rain of heat they waited patiently, each one knowing that a rain of fire would be his if he moved. When the sun was westering and a breeze had come up to rustle the palms and ripple the river water, the white men came out from their shelters and started giving brisk commands which the natives in their employ hastened to carry out. The captives were loaded into long canoes—twenty to a canoe—with a native in the stern to direct the course down stream. A white man in the bow faced the captives with musket loaded and levelled on them.

Manacled and chained to each other, the Atmun-shi did little more than crouch in the boats, the women moaning to themselves. One of them in the rear canoe still held his head unbowed. He was determined to watch the course they were taking so when the time came that they could assert their freedom he would be able to lead his people back to their own village.

The current was swift and the long, narrow, heavily laden canoes moved down it easily. On both banks of the river rose a forest of huge trees from whose tops trailed a network of vines and flowers. Below was the dense undergrowth of the jungle land. Now and again they passed small clearings where flocks of goats grazed and tribesmen watched their goats with more interest than they did the canoes going down the river. At such places, the eye could range inland from the sedgy shore of the river to distant walls of mountains. At-mun, with his keen sight, saw torrents of icy water rushing down rock slopes. Then the trees thickened again. The banks of the river were clothed with giant ferns and mosses. Leaves, large as cloaks, hung down from the trees. Monkeys, chattering in their aerial homes, peered out at the sight of the canoes, and swung from limb to limb to travel with them for awhile. Sometimes, where the river lapped the shore, a hippopotamus lay sunning his great bulk or a crocodile slept with open mouth.

The sun, though it had dropped far down the sky, still had the heat of day and the forest blazed and quivered with its beams. Blossoms of brilliant hue were twice beautiful as they found their reflections in the water. All along the way the land cried out the year's new growth. Reds, yellows, greens were still pale with spring, but under the sun's powerful rays they would soon intensify to the fullness of summer's coloring. More and more as the afternoon wore on, they passed places where the land had been subdued. Furrows had been made in it by tribesmen preparing it for tillage, and stone encampments instead of rude huts could be seen on the hilltops.

At-mun saw it all. It was to him as if he had reached the world's horizon and stepped across it, so different was it to the world he had known— that one small village, hemmed around by the dense growth of the jungle. Hunger gnawed at At-mun, weariness weighted his limbs, and the seam made by the lash on his back ached in the blaze of the sun. But more than all that he felt something expanding within him: a strange feeling that rose to meet the new world his eyes were absorbing. It was as far from elation as it was from fear, yet it was a compound of each. He who had known nothing but the jungle now found wonder stirring in him that there was a world beyond.

Night came and the canoes glided down the

river that was as dark as the sky above. They might have been moving through the sky for the stars that found themselves in the water and the points of light that quivered on the rippling waves. The captives, huddling against each other in what comfort they could in their chains, slept. The white man in the bow propped his musket between his knees and leaned his head forward. The steersman shifted less often. And At-mun, turning his head up to the heavens, prayed to the Spirit of the Night, prayed to the Spirit of the River, prayed to the Spirit of his father. And the voice of the land gave answer. This was the time of birth, the time of renewing. The At-mun-shi were a peaceful people who killed the creatures of the jungle only in their need for food and then burned the entrails in expiation to the Spirit of the victim.

At-mun knew his strength. He knew that he could break the bamboo withes that bound his wrists. He knew that he could kill with his hands. He clenched his hands together. He was the only man awake in the canoe, but his people would waken at a word and they would do his bidding since he was their chief. The other canoes were lost in the darkness before them. Lifting his head again to the sky patterned with stars, he prayed to the God of Life—greater than the Spirit of the Night, older than the Spirit of the River, wiser than the Spirit of his father. And again the voice of the land gave answer, sighing through the tall trees, echoing in bending fern and willowy reed. This was the time of birth, the time of renewal. This was not the time of death. At-mun leaned his head forward on his knees and slept.

Three hours after dawn they reached the place where the river emptied into the sea. Far out on the throbbing water, the At-mun-shi saw a ship with furled sails, riding at anchor. To them it was a great bird sent for their deliverance and in his heart each one hailed it. The canoes were beached and the captives were driven into a line on the shore. Some of the captors waved whips, others brandished guns as they drove the At-mun-shi to the pits. These were a series of holes ten feet deep in the ground and into them the people freed of their shackles were herded. Cocoanuts were split open and tossed into the pits and the people, now almost crazed with hunger, grabbed at them. Coarse loaves followed the cocoanuts and goatskins of water. The captors then laid a rough matting over each pit, rolling heavy stones to the edge to hold the matting in place. Shade from the sun was provided, but such shade offered small protection from the rain. Once a day the matting was drawn away and food was tossed into the pits. And for three weeks the At-mun-shi waited.

But they did not wait alone. From time to time, as more raids were made into the interior, more captives were brought back and thrown into the pits. Some were from tribes the At-mun-shi had known as friendly neighbors. Others were ones against whom they had often defended themselves. Still others were unknown. But differences or similarities mattered little in the pits and even language made small bond. Frightened and angry, the captives milled around in their confinement. They fought for the food thrown down to them and had neither hate nor friendship in common, only an animal instinct to survive, though for what end no one knew.

At-mun tried to hold together those of his people with him in the pit. But as the days passed they seemed less and less able to respond to him and eyes that had once looked at him with reverence looked at him in a daze, then looked away. The time came when the eyes looking into his bore no recognition in their glance.

After three weeks the pits were full and the *White Falcon,* riding at anchor, was impatient to set sail. During the days her small boats had been going back and forth to the mainland securing foodstuffs and laying in stores—corn, beans and yams, fruit, cocoanuts, medicinal herbs and vinegar in hogsheads. Once the stores were full, the master was ready to come ashore to do his business with the white traders. He would soon exchange his cargo of molasses and rum, tobacco and gunpowder for a black cargo of slaves. But only the healthiest and largest, the youngest and ablest of all those gathered in the pits would interest him.

Before the trade was made, the captives were brought up from the pits and fastened together by twos, at ankles and wrists. They were washed and fed well, then their hair was shaved and their bodies oiled. They stood in a long patient row, like animals trained at last to obey commands. The traders were pleased at what the time and treatment in the pits had done. For the African tribesmen and women now were what they wanted them to be—merchandise that could be exchanged for merchandise.

The traders went up and down the line surveying their property.

"That tall fellow there," one said, "should be good for a barrel of rum, no less, or twenty pounds sterling."

"He'd go for more if he wouldn't hold his head up the way he does," another trader answered.

"What the pits didn't do for him the ship will," the first man replied. "He won't be holding his head up when he steps ashore at—where's the *Falcon* from anyway?"

"Boston, but she's going to drop her cargo all along the Atlantic coast. They're needing labor at so many places that she's making half a dozen calls."

A small boat put off from the *White Falcon* and soon the master arrived. Together with the traders he went up and down the line inspecting the black people. Occasionally indicating one he would not take, that one was removed and thrown back into a pit. No one under four feet could meet approval, no one over twenty-five years. The master of the *White Falcon* prided himself on being as shrewd a judge of time as he was of flesh. A score of the finest had been singled out and were standing separately, docile in their chains, heads bowed—all but one—bodies glistening from the palm oil. The master felt their muscle, ran his hand down their thighs, looked into their mouths to see their teeth. Then he turned briskly and went into the tent to do business.

When the papers were signed, a signal was given. The three hundred and forty-five black people who, having won approval, had been bought and paid for were conveyed out to the ship and stowed away in the hold. The head room was so low that they had to stoop to enter. The body room was so narrow that they had to lie spoon fashion, men on one side of the ship, women on the other. Wrists and ankles still chained, they would be given no food until morning. That was part of the discipline of the ship, the mate barked at them, no food unless they behaved. And if they didn't behave then no food and the lash. But the waves slapping against the ship had more meaning than the words shouted through the hatch.

At-mun drew himself up to a sitting position and through a small air chink looked out. The sun was setting. Long lines of light across the water made the distant shore gleam. Mangroves fringed the tawny beaches and cormorants skimmed over the waves. That was his land, At-mun thought, there he had been born and nursed and grown to manhood. There, for a moment of time, he had stood as chieftain of his people. Where the great bird in whose belly they lay would bear them he did not know. One thing he knew, that he looked upon his land for the last time. He called to his people in the At-

mun-shi tongue. There were twenty or more in
the space near him, yet not one of them answered
him. They had been made to forget—not only that
they were At-mun-shi but that they were men.
They made sounds to each other in the darkness of the hold, but they were only sounds, they
had no meaning. All through the night, after the
ship had unfurled her sails and caught the wind
that would bear her on her course, At-mun stayed
awake. He compelled himself to remember as
far back as he could in the past that he might
have something more than his body to carry into
the future.

The Middle Passage took two months—two
months of fair weather, of storms, of calm, of
blistering heat, of cold that came out of the teeth
of the wind. Once a day the Africans were
brought up on deck for an hour. In such freedom as their shackles permitted, they were allowed to move about while their quarters were
cleaned and washed with vinegar. Then the hose
was turned on them and the salt water stung their
naked bodies. They were fed their meager ra-
tions and sent down again, while anything but

utmost docility was punished by the lash. At-mun did not try to talk with his people while they were on deck. The lash would have been his only reward. He was finding it more and more difficult to distinguish his own people since they did not respond to him. It was increasingly hard for him even to remember the life behind him. Dulled by harsh treatment and inactivity, only the present seemed to matter—a little food, water to ease the mouth's dryness, and a return to the dark of the hold from the fierce glare of the sun.

At-mun found that as the days and weeks went by he could recall less and less of his early life. But there were two things that he felt he must burn forever upon his memory—the face of his sister, so he would know her when they met again, and his birthright. "I am a king," At-mun whispered to himself in the At-mun-shi tongue, over and over in the darkness of the hold of the rolling ship, "I am At-mun."

The *White Falcon* made her first stop at the Carolinas, selling a third of her cargo. Her master was satisfied with the crossing. Of the three hundred and forty-five he had started out with, he still had more than three hundred. Disease had not spread among his cargo as it often did on a slave ship, and though some of the blacks had died and a few had thrown themselves overboard, a captain expected such things. Impatiently he moved off a hundred men and women, those most in need of leaving the ship. Bathed, oiled and clothed enough for decency, they made a good sight as they stood on the wharf at Charleston. Then he waited for a high tide and his fee. Fifteen pounds sterling he was asking for every black put ashore, though many of them would bring more when put up on the auction block and well he knew that some of them would never reach it.

The *White Falcon* sailed slowly up the coast. It put in at different ports and dropped off anywhere from fifty to sixty blacks at a time, depending on the need for labor and the price they could fetch. The graceful white-winged bird approached her home port of Boston on the first Sunday in July of the year 1725. The master gave orders to furl sail and ride at anchor outside the harbor until the next day. More than one slaver had been forced to go elsewhere because she had tried to land her cargo on a Sunday.

When the ship drew up to her wharf on Monday morning, twenty slaves—all that remained of her human cargo—were brought up on deck. Among them were the strongest, those least impaired by the voyage and those best able to stand the rugged New England climate. At-mun looked into their faces. Not one of them were of the At-mun-shi. Where his people were now, he did not know.

The gestures, not the words, of the mate made the Africans understand that they were to walk down the gangplank to the wharf. They moved slowly because of their chains, docilely because of the lash that could cut their naked skin as quickly as it could the air. A crowd of people had already gathered near the auction block, men for the most part. But a few curious women hovered on the outskirts. At-mun was hailed by the auctioneer and his chains were removed. For the first time in more than four months he could walk freely, yet not freely. He had been given a pair of trousers to wear before coming off the ship and he found them even more restrictive than chains. The people on the wharf shouted with laughter at the curious way the black youth walked. At-mun mounted the block. Above him, gulls were dipping and soaring, coming to rest in the tall masts of the *White Falcon,* filling the air with their raucous cries. At-mun kept his eyes on them.

"Here's a fine specimen of the Gold Coast," the auctioneer began, slapping At-mun's shoulder and running his hands down the strong arms, the trousered legs. "Well-limbed, not much more than a boy, capable of years of hard work, lusty, strong, sound in health. Remember what you get when you get them young. You can train them the way you want them to go."

A voice shouted out from the crowd.

The auctioneer cupped his ear to hear better. "Defects? Why, none at all. Can't you see for yourself?" Then he consulted a paper the mate had given him describing the *Falcon's* merchandise. "Wait a moment now. It says here that this one can't talk. Is that so?" He peered at

At-mun towering above him and barked up into his face, "Come on, now. Let's hear you say something."

At-mun continued to watch the gulls.

The auctioneer shrugged his shoulders. "That ought to put his price up. Think of having a black who can't talk back to you once he learns English!"

The crowd roared with laughter.

A man dressed in gray and wearing a broad-brimmed hat stepped forward. He looked up at the auctioneer. "What is the youth's name?" he asked.

The auctioneer laughed. "Name? None of them have any names."

The man went to the foot of the block and looked up at At-mun. "What is your name?" he asked.

At-mun had never heard anything come from a white man's lips but commands, curses, threats, none of which he understood. He brought his gaze from the gulls to the face of the man addressing him, for the words just spoken were different in tone. At-mun had no comprehension of their meaning but he understood the look in the man's eyes.   He had never answered a white man.   He had vowed to himself that he never would.   But his lips opened and the word that came through them was "At-mun."

The man in gray turned to the auctioneer. "Friend, will thee take £30 and do no bidding on this man?"

The auctioneer thought for a moment, realizing that he was being offered almost twice what he had hoped to get even with bidding for the truculent black.

"He's yours," he said.

The money was paid and the slave led down from the block.

"He looks an intelligent lad," the purchaser commented.

The auctioneer did not answer until he had pocketed his money.   "That will wear away soon enough," he said.   "Give him plenty of hard work and you'll soon have him in the shape you want him."

"At-mun," the slave said again, wanting to add that he was a king but the words had gone from him. His own name and the dwindling dust of a few memories was all that he had brought with him from his home land.

"Call him Amos," the auctioneer laughed harshly. "That's a good Christian name for a heathen black." He turned and gestured to the next to mount the block.

"Come, friend," the Quaker beckoned to his slave, and the gesture was understood.

"At-mun—" the black mouth opened though no further words came.

"Amos, now," the Quaker said and started away.

So Caleb Copeland, who had not gone to the wharf to buy a slave but to deliver a load of woven cloth, left the wharf with a slave following him and nothing in his pocket from the sale of the woven cloth.

# BOSTON 1725-1740

CALEB COPELAND WAS NOT sure
what he would say to his wife when he arrived
home with no money for the cloth he had taken
with him and a stalwart young Negro boy instead. He need not have feared, for Celia,
his wife, had a generous heart. She hastened to
open the door when she heard the click of the
garden gate.

"How did thee come by the boy?" she asked.
For, tall and dark-skinned as the Negro was, he

had the build of a boy and instantly she thought
he would have been the age of their son had they
not had to wait so long for him to come.

"I bought him at the wharf. A ship had just
come in and they were selling the merchandise."

"Mr. Copeland!" Celia exclaimed, her horror
making her suddenly formal. "Thee knows we
are against slavery."

Caleb sighed. "Yes, and yet when I saw him
standing there and I knew we needed someone to
help in the house, and I knew he would have a
Christian home with kindly treatment and an
opportunity to cultivate his mind, I could not
help buying him. But I bought him outright,
wife. I did not bid on him."

Celia smiled. "He looks a fine strong boy
and you will give him his freedom."

"Yes, in time," Caleb agreed a trifle reluctantly.
"Though in his untamed state it would not be
well to give it him too soon."

"You think he would not know how to use it?"

"He is part animal now. What would he do
but run wild?"

"He looks a good boy to me," Celia remarked.

Amos had stood unmoving during their conversation. But his eyes had been taking in every detail of the house behind the open door and he was not unaware of the small boy and girl who peered out at him from behind their mother's full skirts.

"Yes, I do believe he is a good boy," Caleb admitted. "But none of them sell without some fault and he has a sad one. He cannot speak—"

"Oh, poor lad!" Celia exclaimed. Then she approached him and looked up into his face. "What is thy name, boy?" she asked, as if she would disprove for herself what her husband had just said.

"His name is Amos," Caleb told her.

The boy opened his mouth. "At-mun—" Rich and guttural the sound filled the air, echoing through the house. Then the full lips closed and there was silence.

"That is the only sound he can make," Caleb explained. "He went cheap for that."

"Perhaps he will speak when he has no longer anything to fear." Celia turned briskly and went into the house, feeling that she had other things to do than stand talking on her doorstep, even though it was with her husband. "Take the boy to the work room and show him the trade," she called back, "while I prepare a room for him. Come Roger; come Roxanna," she called to the children, for she had tasks for them.

When she rejoined Caleb and the boy, Caleb was standing by the loom pointing out its operation while the boy stood beside him, head high, face expressionless.

"He doesn't understand anything," Caleb exclaimed, exasperation mounting in his voice as color had to his cheeks.

Celia shook her head. "How can he, poor black lamb. He's heard another tongue all his life. We'll have to teach him." She raised her voice. "Amos," she said, looking at him.

He turned at the sound of her voice. She nodded and said the name again, pointing to him. Then she pointed to Caleb saying his name, and to herself saying hers.

"Amos, come," she said.

He made no move, but his dark face looked more bewildered than stolid.

"Amos, come," she repeated, beckoning this time.

As if drawn by her gesture, he took a step or two toward her. She nodded vigorously. The beginning of a smile flickered over the boy's lips.

Celia looked at her husband. "He will understand in time," she said. "I will teach him as I teach the other children."

She bade the boy come and like an obedient dog he followed her out of the room. She led him to a small plain room off the kitchen. In it was a narrow bed, a chair, a table, all of which meant nothing to the boy. She sat on the chair to show him what to do. He watched her expressionlessly, then, after a moment, he squatted on the floor and grinned up at her.

"Sit," she said slowly, but he made no effort to repeat the word after her.

She lay down on the bed and closed her eyes to indicate sleep. Again he watched her closely, then nodded as he had seen her do. His eyes searched the room and lighted on a woven mat on the floor. Picking up the mat, he folded it carefully in a corner, then curled himself up on it and closed his eyes.

"Sleep," she explained.

He stood up and nodded again. "At-mun," he said, standing taller as he made the sound.

Celia went into the kitchen and the boy followed her. She sat at the long table and gestured to him to do the same. Awkwardly he did so. She put a pewter plate and a fork before him, but when she offered him some food the boy took it in his hands and thrust it into his mouth.

That night, Celia and Caleb Copeland sat together by the fire talking. The children were tucked in their bed and the Negro boy was curled on the mat in a corner of his room.

"It will take time, Caleb, but he is a good boy. He will learn. I think he will even learn to speak."

"But he can make no sound, save that one."

"That is not a sound, Caleb. It is a word. Something he has brought with him from Africa and he will not give it up until he can replace it with something of equal meaning."

"How does thee know that?"

She shook her head. There were some questions that even a good wife could not answer.

It was slow, but Amos learned as a child to do the things about the house that he was shown to do, to help with the carding and spinning, and then, at last, to be trusted with work at the loom. Gradually he relinquished his African ways and sat on a chair, slept on a bed, ate with a knife and fork instead of his fingers. He accustomed himself to trousers and shirt, even seeking a touch of finery in a bird's feather stuck in his hat. He went to Meeting every First Day, sitting in the pew with the Copeland family. He attended the school for children which Mistress Copeland held daily in her spacious kitchen. Roger and Roxanna had been the first pupils, but their mother had made welcome the Negro children who had been born in nearby homes and she taught them all with zeal and devotion.

Amos learned to read and write and cipher, but still he did not speak easily though the expression in his eyes and the mobility of his face spoke for him. From the start he had loved the two

Copeland children, but it was the little girl who seemed to understand him in a special way. Often they sat on the hearth together, Roxanna reading to him from the Bible since that was the book they all read from in their lessons. Amos would listen closely, following with his eyes her finger as it moved across the page.

One day Celia was kneading dough in a corner of the kitchen, not so much listening to as aware of the prattling voice of Roxanna as she read and the answering silence of the Negro.

"You can see for yourself, Amos," the little girl was saying, "the words my father read this morning—'Unto him that loved us, and washed us from our sins in his own blood, and hath made us Kings and priests unto God—'" she laughed, a little ripple of childish pleasure. "Isn't that nice, Amos? You can be a king and I'll be a priest."

There was a silence as Amos bent over the book to see the words. His dark finger traced them and his eyes brought their meaning to him.

Roxanna went on reading.

But Amos, who loved the sound of words, for once was not listening. He had raised his head and was looking before him into the black cavern of the fireplace.

"Then I am a king," he said slowly, and the syllables came between his lips rich and low.

Roxanna looked at him. "You can talk just like me, can't you, Amos?"

He nodded, while he repeated to himself, "I am a king."

"Unto God," the child reminded.

Amos nodded again, then he looked down at the book open in Roxanna's lap. Putting his finger beside hers on the page, they traced the next words and read them aloud together, " 'Behold, he cometh with clouds; and every eye shall see him—' "

The two voices went on murmuringly, slowly, sounding out the words. They read them all no matter how unpronounceable or meaningless, gaining intelligence from them—of one kind to the child, of another to the African.

Celia kneaded her dough quietly as if unaware of the scene on the hearth. But she thought of it often during the days that followed for the strange sound "At-mun" no longer came from

Amos' lips and slowly, haltingly, experimentally he began to join in their conversation. Except for the depth in his voice and the clipt syllabic sound, it was like the voice of Caleb Copeland. Amos was pleased that he could communicate with those near him and he spent more time than ever reading the Bible.

"I am a king," his lips shaped the phrase as lovingly as they once had his name of At-mun.

Amos grew from tall lean boyhood to strong and muscular manhood under the Copeland roof. For fifteen years he shared all the life of the household. Roger learned the weaving trade, married and moved to Acton to establish himself there as a weaver. Roxanna grew to be as tall as her father, as skilled in the work of the house as her mother. Amos thought of himself as one of them and whenever Caleb spoke to him of manumission* he said he did not want it yet.

There were many Negroes known to Amos who had been given freedom and who had found it an even harder lot to bear than servitude. There were those of his friends who so longed for

* formal liberation of a slave.

freedom that they plotted among themselves to gain their release and failing to achieve it became sullen and bitter. And there were some who ran away. But more often than not they were captured and brought back. Amos' heart ached for his African friends who were ill-treated, beaten, forced to marry against their will or kept from marrying those they loved. For them, there seemed little future and no past. Since all that had once been theirs had become clouded in their minds and the white man's world with its toil and indignities was nothing they wanted to call their own. They looked to Amos as more than a welcome friend, for he remembered the land from which they had all come and he would tell them stories of it and sing them songs about it. Listening to him, they thought they remembered the past too, and the present did not seem so barren. But though they looked upon him as a leader, he would not join in their plotting against their white masters or in their plans for escape.

"Wait for the free day," he would urge them, "for it is coming."

It had come in the Copeland household; it was

spreading throughout the Quaker community. Soon there would not be a member of the Society of Friends who would own a slave.

"Servants, be obedient to them that are your masters," was the admonition in most households. But it was not so with the Copelands. Amos had been introduced to Christianity through another text. "Bear ye one another's burdens," were the words most often heard in the household to which Amos had allied himself heart and soul and with all the strength of his powerful body.

"But don't you want your freedom?" Celia would ask Amos time and again.

"No," he would reply, "not yet awhile." He wanted to tell her the reason lying back in his mind, but words would not come to him to convey the haze of memory.

Amos knew many a slave who had been freed, given his article of manumission by a grateful master in return for years of faithful service, and given the tools of a trade so he might set himself up and be on the way to a self-respecting life. But Amos had deep within him the inheritance of the At-mun-shi, of looking up to someone older and wiser as a protector. The white man, in the person of Caleb Copeland, had become such a protector to Amos. Amos looked to him with reverence and loyalty. He did not want his life to be apart from Caleb's in any way. As the working member of the Copeland family, Amos had his own dignity. Apart, he would endure the separateness he knew many of his African friends endured because of their lack of status in the white man's world.

Educated by the white man until they had become well-trained and articulate, baptized into his faith, they still were kept apart. "African corners" were assigned to them in the churches and separate plots in the grave yards. So they tended to form their own groups where they knew they would always be welcome. The houses of the free Negroes became meeting places for all the Negroes in a community. There they would gather, telling their stories and singing the songs whose melodies went further back than memory. Sad songs they were, for the most part. Yet hope filtered through them like the sun through a dark day's clouds as fervently they sang of the joys that awaited them in another world.

After he had learned to read, Amos spent much of his time pouring over the Boston *News-Letter,* reading with special interest of the arrival of ships at the wharf and the discharge of their cargoes. When Caleb Copeland had cloth to be delivered, he granted Amos' wish and let him take it on a day when a sailing ship had arrived.

Amos liked the excitement of the harbor. The air was alive with activity and echoed with shouts as outgoing ships were loaded with rum and fish, textiles and lumber. Incoming ships were unloaded of molasses and sugar, cotton and Negroes. Of these there were never a great number for the bulk had already been sold at high prices in the plantation colonies. The men and the women lined up on the deck or standing in chains on the wharf, Amos scarcely bothered to look at. But to the children he gave his full attention. Almost always there were one or two, sometimes several, for certain ship's masters were renowned for bringing in boys and girls to be trained early

as personal servants. High in hopes Amos went,
watching the little ones frightened or rebellious,
as they were torn from their own people and
stood up on the block.

Amos longed to say a word of comfort or cheer
to them. Yet he knew that few words of the
At-mun-shi remained with him except his own
name. Eyes met eyes while he wondered if anything in his could answer the questions in those
that looked at him. Yet, with the cargo discharged and the auctioneer calling for bids, Amos
would turn sadly away. No small dark girl with
a smile like the first rays of dawn and a useless
leg that she must drag behind her all her life had
come off the ship. He turned home again, remembering, wondering, reaching out to touch
the head of a thin little black boy to ease the ache
in his own heart.

Amos' friends used to call him Mr. Fortunatus
because he had had good fortune in being well
treated. And Amos responded readily to the
name. His friends could use it if they liked, he
thought, for they were not apt ever to see his
back bearing the marks still of the beatings he

had had in the early days. He would not let himself forget those days because he wanted to remember much else connected with them. In time, the name was formalized to Fortune and Amos knew that when the day came and he was Mr. Copeland's Amos no longer he would stand before the world as Amos Fortune, free man. But Caleb Copeland died before he had given his devoted slave his certificate of freedom. A week later a notice appeared in the *Gazette*.

> "To be sold at Public Vendue on Tuesday, 22nd April 1740, at 2 o'clock in the afternoon at the house where the late Mr. Caleb Copeland lived, one weaver's loom and sundry appurtenances, two bedsteads, chairs, tables, a Turkey carpet, various articles of tin and pewter ware, and one likely Negro, in good health, thirty years of age."

Celia had not wanted it to be so. She and Roxanna had wept at the thought of parting with their possessions and their faithful friend. But there were debts to be paid and Amos had comforted them with his assurance of a right outcome for them all. He had not dwelt for half of his lifetime in a Christian household without absorbing trust and confidence. He did not care where he was taken, he told Celia, as long as it was not far inland. But he could not give her his reason and she thought it was because he loved the smell of the sea that he went to so often.

Amos wanted to be able to spend the free time allowed him in haunting the wharfs when ships came in. Though fewer and fewer Negroes were being brought to New England he would keep looking until he found the object of his search— a girl of twelve rainy seasons, a girl who would not bring much at public auction because of the limp with which she walked. Perhaps she would go for so little that he himself could buy her. Thinking of that, Amos would count his hoard of savings, waiting for the day. It was hard to remember her, but he still could make himself see the African village just as it was on that last night —his father, and the small frail Ath-mun, the wooden flutes and the beating drums and the immemorial chant. The sun stood still over Africa, it was only in America that it moved.

The day of the vendue came and the household articles and weavers' tools sold well. Amos sat

on the bench on which he had sat for all his lessons until it was sold out from under him. Then
he stood by the auctioneer. It amused him to
hear himself described and he grinned broadly as
he listened to the auctioneer's words.

"This likely fellow, strong, healthy, thoroughly
domesticated, speaks English better than I do.
He's a weaver by association with Mr. Caleb
Copeland but he's smart enough to learn any
trade. He's a rare offering in these days. What
will you give me for him?"

"Ten Pounds," a voice spoke out from the
crowd.

The auctioneer laughed. "He would cost
more than that on the Gold Coast. This isn't the
raw untamed product, my good man, but something highly civilized."

The bids crackled out, mounting up. Amos
even bid once on himself and a roar of laughter
went up from the crowd. When the bidding
went over £50, Amos withdrew. He could not
spend that much and have anything left for Ath-
mun when she came. The bidding stopped at

£62, and the last sum was offered by the man who had made the first bid.

"Sold to Mr. Ichabod Richardson, Tanner, of Woburn," the auctioneer bellowed out, "one black slave, by name Amos Fortune, for the consideration of Sixty-two Pounds Sterling."

A half hour later Amos rode off with Mr. Richardson in his wagon. He had said good-by to the house that had been his home for his first fifteen years in America. He had promised to write to Mrs. Copeland and he had said he would not forget her. He did not know what lay before him, but he had the omen in his name to fall back on. He had had good fortune. He would have it again.

Ichabod Richardson levelled his eyes on his black companion, erect of back, head high. "I think I know a good thing when I see it," he said. Then he clucked to the horse and they clattered over the road on their way to Woburn.

# WOBURN 1740-1779

❧ ICHABOD RICHARDSON WAS a good man, inclined to be stern and with a leaning toward silence. He had had slaves before and he prided himself on knowing how to treat them: teach them a trade through the week, make Christians of them on Sunday, pay them—not what he would a white man but what he deemed a just consideration for their service, and give them their freedom before they became too old to enjoy it. When the end of the day came and they had reached the village of Woburn, though few words had been exchanged during the journey, Ichabod Richardson, tanner, and Amos Fortune, chattel, knew enough about each other to know that they would work well together.

Mr. Richardson went into the house where he was greeted by his wife and family. Amos led the horse to the barn and cared for it. Then he returned to the house. Briefly the master tanner showed the slave apprentice his living quarters and told him to be in the kitchen for prayers and the morning meal at half after five the next day. Amos seemed loathe to leave so Mr. Richardson asked him if there was anything about the work he wanted to know before morning. Amos smiled and shook his head, then he asked the question that had been foremost in his mind all day.

"Thank you, sir," he said respectfully, and then more boldly. "I'll ask you to tell me when your paper advises you of a ship in from Africa at the Boston wharf. If you'd be sending some leather to Boston I'd like to take it on that day."

Mr. Richardson clicked his teeth. "There are

nothing like the number of slave ships coming in now that there used to be, Amos, but I'll let you know when I hear of one." Then severity tightened his lips. "But you'll have that privilege only on good behavior."

Amos flashed a knowing smile. If he understood one thing clearly it was that: that no good came to a slave except as a reward for his behavior. He took the candle from Mrs. Richardson's outstretched hand and the plate of food she had ready for him, then he went across the grass to the hut that was Mr. Richardson's workshop and would be Amos' home all the years of his servitude. From the house, Ichabod Richardson and his wife heard the slave singing to himself long after he had blown out his candle to save the precious tallow.

Mrs. Richardson tilted her head to listen. "If you had a slave for no other reason than their singing, I often think it would be worth it," she said. "And yet, so long as they're not free their songs are like those of birds in a cage."

"He'll have his freedom in time, but not until he's paid me well for the price I paid for him."

The years went on and Amos learned the trade
of a tanner.  He worked well with the hides and,
as in the kindly Quaker household in Boston, he
soon made himself an indispensable part of the
Richardson family.  He fulfilled Mr. Richardson's requirement to profess Christianity, thereby
justifying in large measure the expenditure Mr.
Richardson had made.  Amos went to church for
two long hours in the morning and again in the
afternoon, observing with respect the laws that
pertained to the Sabbath during the hours when
he was not under the vigilant eye of the minister.
It puzzled Amos that the white people put so
much stress on Sunday.  Yet it seemed somehow
similar to the stress they put on the color of a
man's skin.  To Amos, once he understood the
Lord, every day was lived to Him.  It was not in
the Meeting House alone but in the tan yard
that he took delight in being a Christian.  It was
not with his own people he felt at his best but
with all men.  He was to go to the end of his days
without fully understanding the white man's attitude to the color of a man's skin.  But it did not
trouble or vex him the way it did some of the

other slaves with whom he met and talked. It puzzled him. But then, there were many things to puzzle a man. And as the years went on there were more, for they were years fraught with the excitement of great events.

The Colonies were seething with the rush of bold ideas. As taxation grew more unjust and the long arm of authority wielded across an ocean grew more tyrannical, liberty became the word that warmed the people's hearts and fired the tongues of their spokesmen. The new country that had established itself with such eager rapidity was feeling more sure of itself. In the strength that had been born and tested through the subduing of a wilderness, it had begun to dare to assert its independence.

From time to time Mr. Richardson would read in the *Gazette* or the *News-Letter* the advice of a ship soon to arrive at Boston harbor with "human merchandise." Remembering his agreement with Amos, he would send his slave with a cartload of leather to Boston on the day of the ship's arrival. It was no hardship for him to part with his slave for such a purpose, for he had early learned that

Amos could drive a better bargain than he could. For some time he had been letting Amos do all the selling of the leather. With his permission to Amos to be at large for a day, he gave him a written paper stating to any who might be concerned the nature of the slave's business. Were Amos delayed and seen on the streets after nine at night without such a paper, he would be whipped by the constable no matter what explanation he might offer.

Amos did not rely solely on the advices in the papers, he watched the advertisements as well. These were often for single slaves to be sold privately or at auction. He made notations in the small book he always carried on his person of those he would see on his next time in Boston. One advertisement interested him especially:

Three Negro Men and Two Women
to be sold and seen at the House of
Mr. Josiah Greenwood in Center Street

Houses and taverns were often used as show-rooms for human chattels and Amos preferred seeing them in such places. He went to the house in Center Street and tried to talk to the five Africans waiting patient and stolid for the exchange of money that would give them a home and occupation. But they knew no words of English and Amos had few words of the At-mun-shi tongue even had they once spoken it. It was his continuing sorrow that he had not been able to hold more of his early speech in memory. Once he had learned to write English he had tried to recall certain words of the At-mun-shi so he might record them for himself, but they were not there. Search through his mind as he might, and with all the longing of his heart, they were not there.

The dark faces of the Africans sitting in Mr. Josiah Greenwood's kitchen looked at him. Amos held out his hand to them, trying to tell them in some way that their new life might yet be happy. But their faces remained impassive, and Amos thought that even though they might understand him they would not believe him. Most Africans had already suffered so much at the hands of white men that they regarded every white man as an enemy.

Amos never pursued an advertisement that spoke only of Negro men or boys, for he was not interested in them. Always he was looking for a young girl whose voice ranged like a bird's though her limbs would carry her at no more than a snail's pace. An advertisement describing "A Negro woman, nineteen years, and her infant, six months, to be sold either together or apart" attracted Amos. But when he saw the woman she was not beautiful as Ath-mun had been. She was sullen and silent, though she had been in the country several years and her former master declared her English to be tolerably good.

On the same day Amos traced yet another advertisement: "Selling for cash or short credit, a Negro Wench about eighteen years of age, strong and healthy, used to all kinds of work indoors and out. The above Wench is sold for no fault of her own, the owner at present having no employ for her." But when he saw her he knew she was not the one he was seeking.

So Amos returned to Woburn with the money for the leather and news for Mr. Richardson of what was doing at the wharfs and in the taverns. And always be brought some small trinket for Mrs. Richardson. One time it was a mirror made of highly polished tin. It was the finest present Amos had ever brought to her and he did it for two reasons—one because it caught his eye and the other because he was soon to be promised his freedom. Twenty years and more he had done the work of a tanner, grown as a member of the household and satisfied Ichabod Richardson. That knowledge, as well as the air he breathed, gave him the boldness to ask for his freedom rather than to wait indefinitely upon Mr. Richardson's will.

On a December evening in 1763 he made a bargain with his master, agreeing to all Mr. Richardson's reasonable conditions but insisting that six years from that date he was to be a free man. When all was agreed to, Amos took from inside his shirt the polished tin sheet and handed it to Mrs. Richardson. A piece of finery it was, of vanity that might have been scoffed at by many New England housewives but that all would value nonetheless, even though true enjoyment of it might only come in secret. She stood it against a candle stick, standing away to see herself in it. It was a quiet face and a kind face that smiled back at her in the soft tallow glow; but, so no one could accuse her of vanity, she spoke quickly.

"Ah, Amos, I'm not the same person that I was when you first came here."

"Some folks only grow more beautiful," Amos smiled.

"But we all grow older," Mrs. Richardson said warningly. "Why, even you, Amos—see for yourself."

So Amos stood before the sheet and saw his own face—black and strong, eyes bright, teeth white, close cropped hair showing gray. Fifty years had rolled over him and though muscles and brawn could do the work they had always done, and hope still led him on, time had left its mark. Then the gay smile flickered from his face and the flash in his eyes went out as he put his hands across them to take away what he had seen. Not his own face but Ath-mun's had looked at him from the polished tin. Long and lovingly as he had sought her, he had not found her because always he had been seeking for a young girl. The years had done no less to Ath-mun than they had to him: she had become a woman as he had become a man.

A sob wracked him. He turned to Mrs. Richardson and looked at her for a moment with eyes that like snuffed candles had no light in them. Then putting his hands across his face again he stumbled out of the room. They heard him late that night singing in the darkness of the tannery—

"You got to cross that river Jordan,
You got to cross it for yourself;
O there can't nobody cross it for you,
You got to cross it for yourself;
Can't your brother cross it for you,
You got to cross it for yourself."

"What happened to him?" Ichabod Richardson asked.

"I don't know," his wife replied. "Amos looked at himself in that little mirror he brought me and at first his image seemed to delight him. Then it affected him strangely."

"Perhaps he thought he was white until he saw himself in the mirror."

Mrs. Richardson shook her head. "Perhaps,

but it's more than that. There's a yearning in him that has its roots in the land from which he came. Oh, it's a terrible thing we've done, Mr. Richardson, to bring these black people to our land and treat them as we do."

"Their lot's not too hard," he remonstrated.

"Ah, but until they're given their freedom they count no more than cattle."

Ichabod Richardson sighed deeply. "They're not the only ones to be thinking about freedom. Before many more years have passed we'll be thinking about it too, and not as people but as a nation."

"What do you mean, Mr. Richardson?"

"I mean that we've made others slaves readily enough but we'll be slaves ourselves if we don't keep watch."

While Amos sang to comfort himself, Ichabod Richardson drew up the paper that would mean the ultimate freedom of his slave. As he wrote, he was buoyed by a sense of generosity and uprightness. "Know all men by these presents," his quill made a graceful flourish with the final letter, "that I, Ichabod Richardson, of Woburn in the

county of Middlesex and province of the Massa-
chusetts-bay in New England, Tanner, for diverse
good reasons me hereunto especially moving have
and by these presents do covenant promise, grant
and agree to, and with my negro man Amos, that
at the end of four years next insuing this date (or
at my decease if it should fall within that term)
that he, the said Amos, shall then be discharged,
freed, and set at liberty from my service, power
and command forever, and have full liberty to
trade, traffick and dispose of himself in all re-
spects as he pleases, and have and enjoy and
convert to his own use all the profit of his own
labor and industry, equal to men that are free-
born, and that neither I, nor my heirs, nor any
other person, or persons acting or claiming by
or under me or them shall have challenge, or
claim any right to, or in his person property or
labors, but therefrom shall be excluded and forever declared by force and virtue of these presents.
In witness whereof I, the said Ichabod Richardson, have hereunto set my hand and seal the
thirtieth day of December 1763 in the fourth year
of His Majesty's reign——"

It was late when Mr. Richardson finally snuffed the candle and put on his nightcap, but his wife was wakeful and waiting for him in the double bed with its heavy hanging curtains. He told her of all that he had done and she smiled with relief in the darkness that her husband had at last made sure the freedom of his faithful slave.

"I shall talk with Simon Carter in the morning," Ichabod said, "and Amos shall pay to him the full indenture. He's a banker and will take care of it as a trust fund so in case Amos is unable to work at any time, due to sickness, you and the children will be cared for."

"Then are pounds and pence paid by Amos himself your 'diverse good reasons'?" his wife questioned.

"With certainty."

"You are a hard man, Ichabod Richardson," she said quietly. She had said it before in silence. She voiced it now in words.

Amos was pleased the next morning when he was shown the paper, and the fact that he would have to buy his own freedom by paying an agreed sum for the next several years to Mr. Carter did not dilute his pleasure. He could look ahead to a future of freedom, achieved by his own efforts and not through the kindness of any man.

It was well that Amos Fortune's freedom was established for the paper granting it survived Ichabod Richardson. Soon after the tanner's death, Mrs. Richardson saved Amos further investment in his freedom by a quitclaim of her interest in the fund into which Amos was paying. She drew up a paper of her own, brief and clear, in which she said, "In consideration of the many faithful services Amos Fortune did perform to the said deceased Ichabod in his lifetime and hath since performed to us respectively whereby our several interests have been greatly increased, I do grant unto Amos Fortune the full and free liberty of his person from and after the ninth day of May, 1769."

It was a strange thing to wake up on that morning of the ninth of May and know that he was a free man. Amos took the paper out of his pocket and read it again to assure himself, then he returned it to his pocket. It was a paper that he would carry on his person until the day of his death. He tidied his small room and did up his affairs in a bundle. He had no more than he could carry on his back—his Bible, a change of garments, and a pair of silver buckles that he wore on his shoes on Sundays. Then he stood in the doorway and breathed the air that was sweet with blossom and alive with birdsong, and it seemed that now he was free he could breathe more deeply. He watched swallows swooping in their flight, feeling as if he were one of them; his eyes dwelt on a tree that was a mass of white blossom.

It had been spring, too, when he had been free before. The new strength of the sun with which he had matched his strength had been at hand; the growing of the year with which he would grow had been ahead. Yet that had been a lifetime ago; another life, perhaps, for now his life was beginning again. He was almost sixty years old and he was ready to live. He flexed his muscles; they were strong. He raised his head from the blossoming tree to the blue sky above and the thought of Moses came into his mind, of Moses who stood upon Mount Nebo seeing with his eyes the land that his feet might not tread upon.

" 'And Moses was an hundred and twenty years old when he died.' " Amos spoke the words as reverently as if he were reading them from the open book. " 'His eye was not dim, nor his natural force abated.' " That was true for him, he thought. "So there's time for Amos too," he murmured. Time—the same for him as it was for Moses, because for them both there was something to live for. When a man had that he could go on for a long time.

Amos crossed the small garden he had set out and cared for to the house to say good-by to Mrs. Richardson. She was busy with the morning meal, but at sight of Amos she ceased what she was doing.

"Where are you going, Amos?" she asked.

"I don't know, ma'am. Somewhere that I can work and establish a home."

"It's only half a home without a wife. Have you thought of anyone, Amos?" She gestured to his place at the table.

Setting his bundle down, Amos drew up to the table as he had for years past. "Indeed I have and when I've saved up my money again I'll buy her and make her mine."

"Again, Amos?" then Mrs. Richardson blushed. Well she knew that Amos' hard earned savings had all gone to buy his own freedom. Even the date of manumission set by her husband—four years from the document drawn up in 1763—had meant nothing because of the sum he had stipulated between himself and Amos. Toward that sum Amos would have been paying yet had she not drawn up her own document.

Then Mrs. Richardson told Amos of the plan she had been considering, that he work on at the tannery and slowly establish it as his own.

Amos smiled with delight, but he had his own pride and he would accept nothing without fair payment. He agreed to work on with the tools and the vats he had been handling for years past while he built his own home and business and then settled himself.

It took Amos four years to establish his trade and build a homestead for himself, but by then he was accepted as a citizen of Woburn. He worked during the day, saving a few hours off when he would leave the tanning and become carpenter on his own account. Every evening, except Sunday, during the fourth year he presented himself at the kitchen door of the house of Jonathan Twombly and asked to see Lily.

Lily had been a slave for forty years, sometimes faring well, often ill, at the hands of her many masters. Amos had met her years ago at one of the African gatherings. From the first he had loved her, but he would not let himself think of her as a wife until in asking her hand in marriage he could offer her freedom. Lily would have married him as a slave and it would not have been out of keeping in the Twombly household to have allowed her to marry while still retaining her as a slave. But Amos would not have it so.

"We'll wait a while," he said to her comfortingly. "We blacks are used to waiting."

And Lily, loving Amos and trusting him in everything, agreed to wait.

The tide of events was rolling on. Much of the world was thrilled, some of it stood aghast when on a December day in 1773 tea was dumped in Boston Harbor because the colonists refused to pay a tax when they had no representation in Parliament. But another event had happened in that same year though it caused no furor. A petition had been presented to the Massachusetts Legislature by a group of Boston Negroes deploring the severance of families through sale. Even the despised slave was becoming vocal. The wind of freedom that was passing over the world left nothing untouched. Wherever there was oppression, something began to stir. When the end would be no one knew, but it was bound to result in the right of every man to be free.

Talking of such things in the warmth of the big kitchen Amos would repeat, "We've still a while to wait."

One day, toward the end of the fourth year, Amos presented himself at the front door of Mr. Twombly's house, asking to see Mr. Twombly himself.

He was ushered in to the gentleman's presence, though he would go no further than the entrance to the room. Standing in the doorway and holding his beaver hat in his hands, he made his request known.

"I'd like to buy your Lily," he said quietly. "I have the money."

Mr. Twombly looked at him sharply. "Lily is still worth £20 to me," he said, and then added, "that's the price I paid for her when I bought her seven years ago."

Amos counted out £20 and handed the notes to the surprised Mr. Twombly before he could change his mind or raise his price.

After Mr. Twombly had pocketed the money, he asked Amos what he wanted the woman for.

"I want to marry her."

"She won't make you much of a wife," he laughed harshly. "She's been ailing the past year. She may not have long to live."

"Then she can die free," Amos said as he bowed and left the gentleman's presence and went out to find Lily: his now, and a free woman because she was his.

Lily died within the year but Amos had the satisfaction of knowing that she died free. And in that October of 1775 freedom was the byword of every American. But even while Lily was his wife, Amos thought of Ath-mun—now only a faint frail part of memory but still dear. He hoped that in making one black woman free he had made Ath-mun free if she was in need of freedom.

On a raw day during the winter when Amos was delivering a load of leather to the house of Josiah Bowers in nearby Billerica, he accepted the cook's invitation to stop by the kitchen hearth for a bowl of soup while he waited for Mr. Bowers' return for his pay. There were servants and slaves around the hearth and Amos felt in good company, listening to their stories, telling his own, joining into songs together. None sang more liltingly nor laughed more sweetly than the black woman, Lydia. But when she rose to leave the kitchen in answer to a bell, she dragged herself across the floor with the aid of a crutch. After she had left the room, silence fell on the group around the hearth.

"You've got big eyes for Lydia, old man," the cook said.

"How is it she's so lame?" Amos asked, almost whispering the words.

"She wasn't always lame," the cook replied.

"They broke her legs in the ship coming over. She hasn't walked right since. But she's Mrs. Bowers' sewing woman and she doesn't need legs for that."

"Is she married?" Amos asked.

"Laws no," the cook exclaimed. "Who ever would marry Lydia!"

When Mr. Bowers returned, Amos was called in to see him. After he had been paid for the leather, Amos said respectfully that he would like to transact some business of his own.

"And what is it?" Mr. Bowers asked, wondering what he had that the Negro had taken a fancy to.

"Your slave, Lydia," Amos said. "I want to buy her."

Josiah Bowers thought for a moment. "I can't sell her cheap. She's a well-trained servant. She can cook and sew and she has a good disposition which is high in her favor."

"She is lame," Amos said.

"She can be yours for £50."

"Is that agreed between us?" Amos asked.

"If you wish it so and if you have my price."

"I do, and I will have in time," Amos said as solemnly as if he were taking an oath.

"But what do you want her for? Her kind of needlework won't be of any use in your trade and she's as lame as a spavined horse."

"I want to marry her."

Josiah Bowers laughed tolerantly. "They say there's no accounting for the whims in a man's heart."

Amos, sure of his part of the bargain, put his beaver hat on his head, buttoned his great coat and went on his way back to Woburn. The flame of hope that had leapt up in him at his first sight of the limping black woman had soon gone out, but the wind did not blow as cold as it had earlier in the day.

It took Amos three years to save up the sum for Lydia—three years during which a war was in the fighting and victory long in coming. The struggling colonies had been bound together by words on a parchment, words that said "All men are created equal . . ." words that were to become the foundation stone of a nation, words easily ascribed to in the enthusiasm of youth when they signified breaking the bonds of restriction and tyranny, words hard to explain to the black man who looked to the white for wisdom and understanding.

Many of Amos' friends joined the ranks of the colonists, fighting well and fearlessly. Some of them gave their lives on the battlefield. There was no difference then in the blood that poured from severed veins, that of a black man or a white could water as well the soil from which freedom was growing. Of the blacks who survived the fighting, many were given their own freedom as a reward for service. Amos longed to be with them. But what was a man far advanced in his sixties to do? Offer his services as he might, prove his strength as he could, yet always he was told—

"Too old for the rigors of a battlefield, the hardships. Too old. Too old."

Yet Amos knew he was never too old to wage his own war for freedom in his own way, not with guns or valor but hard-earned coinage, buying manumission and giving it before it was too late for one he loved to die in honor. Freedom was in the air no less than it was in Amos' blood. It had been his tradition, something vital as his own heart beats. He could not explain how such an intensity of feeling came to him. He knew only that it was there.

Once every week, during the three years he worked to earn the sum for Lydia's freedom, he drove his cart to Billerica and sat in the kitchen with Lydia, talking to her when the other servants were there or long after they had left them alone. A glow came over his face when he told her that he wanted to make her free.

She put her hand in his, smiling up at him. "I never thought I would know freedom. What is it like, Amos? Is the air sweeter to breathe? Is the sun warmer?"

"Can't you remember what it was like in Africa?"

She shook her head. "No, only the voyage. We were so wretched. We tried to escape. Even the ocean would have been better. Some of us did—" she put her hands to her eyes—"I can see them now, jumping into the water that meant freedom. I tried it but—but we who did not escape—they broke our legs. I can't remember anything, Amos, after that but the pain and the long dark days and nights. They never let us out of the hold again and I saw no day until it was in this land."

They were alone in the kitchen and she put her head on his shoulder and sobbed as if the tears she had not wept for twenty years were coming at last. He sang to her softly, and he told her what he could remember about Africa, and Lydia smiled. Six days would have to pass, she thought to herself, before he would be sitting with her again in the kitchen, and yet they would be six days nearer to the time when they would be always together.

Amos had no other thought than to pay the full price. He would not bargain over human flesh nor was it for him to question Mr. Bowers' decision. When the day came that he could call for Lydia in the cart, he presented himself first to Mr. Bowers. In the presence of witnesses,—one who was a friend of Josiah Bowers, and one of the household servants who was Amos Fortune's friend, the money was counted carefully out. Mr.

Bowers set it aside, then he handed to Amos the necessary confirmation of the transaction. It was another bit of paper that Amos would treasure all the days of his life.

> BILLERICA JUNE YE 23 1778
> Then received of Amos Fortune Fifty Pounds in full for a Negro Garle named Lydia Somerset being now my property the which I do sell and convey to the aforesaid Amos and I do covenant with the same Amos that I have just and lawful rite to sell and convey the said Lydia in manner aforesaid and I will warrant and defend the said Lydia to him against all the lawful claims and demands of all persons whatsoever.
> Sined Sealed and Delivered
> in presence of her
>
> > *Milesent Braddon*
> > *Isaac Johnson*
> > *Josiah Bowers*

To Amos it was a cherished possession and it was to live far longer than Lydia. Freedom was almost too sweet for her and she enjoyed it for only a year. Amos was beside her bed when she died. He was happy in the confidence that she had gone forward as a free woman.

# JOURNEY TO KEENE 1779

⊂⋑ ON A MILD JUNE DAY in 1779
Amos Fortune rode the remaining miles between
Woburn and Keene, New Hampshire. Two
days he had been on his way, but on this third
day he knew that he would reach his destination
by nightfall. He had a good horse under him
and strapped to his saddle a bundle of his finest
leather, and he was a free man. No matter where
his thoughts ranged as he jogged over the road,
he kept coming back to that. Even though he

had had his freedom now for just a month over ten years, it was still a treasure to be brought forward in his mind and meditated on with delight. A strange thing freedom was, he thought, with its side of shadow as well as of light. For he was free too of household cares and domestic ties and that saddened him, but only as a passing cloud dims the sun for a moment.

All during the years of his servitude he had longed for the sweetness of a home with a woman in it, but though he had been twice married he had known that with both Lily and Lydia the sweetness could not last for long. With Violet he thought that it would be different for she was younger than he and strong. But she was a slave and he could have her only at the purchase price. James Baldwin had put that price at Fifty Pounds and Amos Fortune had had to glance down the years to see the work he must do to amass that much money.

The purchase price for Violet included Violet's little daughter Celyndia, and Amos was pleased to think that one deed would give freedom to two people. Celyndia was four years old, dusky, sweet-voiced, and in her young eyes Amos saw back into another lifetime. For Celyndia to grow now in freedom would mean so much. To live on in bondage might mean the acceptance of barriers, perhaps, for all her days. Amos had Ten Pounds' worth of leather with him. There was more work in his shop in Woburn that had been done and could be delivered. It might not be far away, that purchase price of Fifty Pounds.

"Easy now, Cyclops," he murmured, stroking his horse, "and we'll both have a rest at the top."

Cyclops slowed to a walk and Amos thought of Joshua and the promised land and of how the Lord told him to be strong and of a good courage. He was like Joshua, he thought, for he too was seeking a new place to live and work, a place where he might build a home for Violet and Celyndia and they three might have such peace as was their portion. When he came to the top of the hill he thought of Joshua no longer but of Amos and his promised land, for spread before him was an area that represented all he could hope for happiness.

There was a clearing and a collection of houses

with a sturdily built Meeting House which faced a mountain rising up in rocky lonely splendor in the west. Face to face they were, the mountain and the house of God: two strong things, both pointing up.

He loosed the reins so Cyclops could feed on the grass along the roadside and he slid off the saddle to stand on his own two feet. His eyes swept the green fields flowing down from the hillside and up the mountain slope dotted with sheep and cattle. A sudden impulse that went far back into his past came over him and he knelt down to press his lips to the earth. When he stood up again he held his hat in his hand and looked at the mountain.

"I've asked You for a sign, Lord, manys the time, and You've always given me one. I'm asking You now. It doesn't need to be anything big, Lord, I'll understand. If this is the place for me to start my life again, I'll thank You kindly for telling me so. Not right away, Lord, but when it's convenient for You. Just sometime before I start the journey back to Woburn." He waited respectfully for a moment in case the sign should come soon, then he picked up Cyclops' reins and mounted into the saddle.

Amos Fortune went on his way singing. The cleared land gave again to forest and his voice echoed through the woodland, merging with the singing of birds, the running of a brook, the clopping of a horse's hooves.

His voice rolled out full and strong. He passed a sign post at a crossroad and the hand that pointed over the road he had come said JAFFREY, six miles, while the hand pointing ahead said KEENE, ten miles. He said the name Jaffrey over and over to himself, whispering it, singing it, speaking it, and every time it was as if he had entered his promised land.

Cyclops was old, though he was a robust horse, and the fact that he had only one eye made Amos easy on him. He had been a poor piece of horse-flesh when his owner had brought him to the tannery and asked Amos how much he would give for his hide. Amos had replied he would give him Two Pounds for the horse alive and the deal had been closed with the exchange. A summer in pasture, good care and something more than care, and the old horse took a new hold on life and was ready to give Amos service.

When Amos Fortune reached Keene he found stabling for Cyclops at the Inn, but no lodging for himself. He shared the stall with his horse, pleased that the straw was clean and there was fresh water at hand to wash down the bread he had brought in his pack. Early in the morning he paid the shilling asked for the horse's accommodation. It was excessive but Amos knew that he could not question the white man's price. Too often ill feelings were vented on a black man for no reason other than his color and his inoffensiveness. Angry words could ensue and then the suspicion would be cast that the man might be a runaway slave. But against such occurrences Amos carried on his person the certificate of his own manumission.

He went on his way to seek Mr. Samuel George to whom the leather was consigned. Finding him in his cobbler's shop on the south side of the town, Amos opened his packet and unrolled the leather before him. The cobbler had always prided himself on having a sharp eye for a flaw, but no matter how closely he examined Amos Fortune's work he could find nothing wrong with it. He shook his head slowly, but the gesture gave Amos no concern. It was a gesture of approval and the tanner recognized it as such.

"I'm wishing we had a tanner such as you somewhere near," Mr. George said.

"You've got a tanner down by the river," Amos commented.

"I said 'such as you,'" Mr. George reminded him. He stroked the leather with his hands. It was smooth and supple. The best that was in the hide had been coaxed from it by knowing hands. Samuel George looked closely at the freed Negro facing him and he thought that though the man had the look of being familiar with time he bore none of the marks that time could leave. He was well built and well muscled, carrying his head high. There was gray in his hair, but his face was furrowed more by laughter than by years.

There was a twinkle in Amos' eyes when he asked, "How far would a man travel to get his hides tanned—ten miles?"

Samuel George laughed. "That's not half a day's journey! Why man, if you were to settle anywhere in this countryside you'd have people bringing their hides to you from miles around."

When it came to paying out the money for the leather Samuel George was slow in making the transaction. As he placed the last note in Amos' hand he said, "It's good your leather costs no more for I've come to the end of my money until my customers pay me."

Amos folded four of the notes carefully away, but he held out six and said thoughtfully, "Would you like to have some of it on credit?"

The cobbler looked like a hungry man being offered food. "I'd like to borrow some of those notes back again if you're willing. I'll offer any security you like."

Amos' eyes roved the small shop with its tools of trade, its boots and shoes. Then he looked at Samuel George, ample in girth in middle years. There might be some clothes he could no longer wear which would hang nicely on Amos' leaner build.

"How about your go-to-Meeting hat," Amos

began tentatively. "Would you want to part with it now?"

The cobbler laughed. "You've chosen the one thing I've no more use for." He crossed the room to a press and took from it a fur hat which looked as if it had not seen the light of a Sunday morning for a long time. He drew out a broadcloth coat and a patterned jacket with a stripe that was the same blue as the coat.

"Here," he said. "You might as well take the lot. I've grown too big for them. Take them as security."

"Or in sale?" Amos asked.

"Either will suit me," Samuel George concluded, relieved to have six pound notes when he thought he was down to a few pence and glad to have his press cleared of useless clutter.

A half hour later, when Amos went down the road on Cyclops with his newly acquired garments in a neat bundle on the saddle, his fur hat on his head, Samuel George smiled to himself as he watched him go.

"What he wants with all those fine clothes is hard to see," he said aloud to himself. "They caught his fancy like a child's. But that's what they are, those black people, nothing but children. It's a good thing for them the whites took them over."

In retracing his way, Amos stopped again on the hill that was Jaffrey. He faced the mountain he was leaving behind and talked to it as a man might to a friend.

"I'll be back," he said. "Just you wait there, you old mountain, and we'll soon be talking together every day." Then he lifted his gaze a little higher and looked skyward. "Thank You kindly, Lord, for the sign You gave me back there in Keene, and thank You for all my fine clothes. Violet's going to be mighty proud when she sees me in them, but I'll keep them for our wedding day—her freedom day, so help me, Lord."

It was November before Amos had the money ready for his purchase and on the ninth day he went to the house of James Baldwin where Violet was a domestic and Celyndia, for all her few years, was made to do more than a child's duties. An hour later they walked out of the house to-

gether, the little girl following them. And the
next day they went to the church to be married.
Violet wore the simple homespun dress she had
made herself and Amos wore the broadcloth coat
and gay jacket he had secured in Keene. The
church register was signed—

*Amos Fortune and Violet Baldwin, blacks,
both of Woburn      November 10, 1779*

The vows were made, the ring slipped on and
they left the church to begin their united life.

Violet took in deep breaths of freedom and
Celyndia ran ahead, chasing a small bird. The
world belonged to them. Violet was no longer
at the beck and call of a white man who would
have her do his bidding. She was her own master now. She smiled at Amos. He had given
her his love and her freedom. She had no words
with which to thank him, but deep in her heart
she prayed that she might be his true helpmeet
during the years remaining to them both.

Celyndia came running back to them as the
bird flew off across a meadow, dipping to the
grass, then soaring to a bush's height, balancing

itself against the wind as it pursued some pattern of its own.

"Why'nt you go on fluttering after the flutterling, child?" Violet asked.

" 'Cause he flew over that field and we can't go there."

"The world is yours, Celyndia," Amos said quietly. "Don't you remember what I told you last night? You're as free as the birds in the air."

A smile started to part Celyndia's full lips, but before it had its way the lips began to quiver and the large dark eyes filled with tears. Amos stooped down to be on her level and she threw her arms around his neck.

"That's a strange thing for that child to do," Violet said apologetically. "She's getting your fine jacket all spotted."

"Let her alone, Violet," Amos said as he patted Celyndia's heaving shoulders, "some things are too wonderful even for a child, and freedom's one of them."

# THE ARRIVAL AT JAFFREY

❧ AMOS HAD MORE than a year's work before him to finish the hides in his care. Once they were delivered and paid for he would have in hand a sum sufficient to tide him over the intervening time between the end of his tanning operations in Woburn and the start of them again in Jaffrey. He would need to have a little extra, he realized. Unless he could be paid in advance he would have no money coming to him for six months at least, since tanning was so slow a process. He knew he could not expect anyone to pay an unknown workman in advance. So he labored diligently and lived frugally that he might accumulate the money for his needs.

It was important for Amos to arrive in his new surroundings in early spring, for the tanbark which was essential to his work had to be removed from trees soon after the sap had risen. With Violet's help and, what was even more, the sure comfort of her presence, he managed to deliver the last of his leather in late March of the year 1781. Then, working together, they packed up all the transportable tools—spud, barking mallet, rollers, knives, even the beam and work table. The vats that could not easily be moved were sold, as was the small house Amos had built himself. A cart was purchased in which they stored the tools and as many household goods as could be carried.

"An ax and a bag of beans is what a man most needs when he sets out for the wilderness," Amos said as he placed them under his seat where he could get at them.

Violet shivered a little at Amos' easy talk of

the wilderness. The comfort of a big house and the companionship of many servants and slaves had been her environment for years past. But she dared not think back on that too longingly. To be with Amos wherever his life might lead him was where her heart would have her. So it was with full confidence in him and undivided affection that she climbed up beside him on the seat of the cart and started over the road to Jaffrey on an April morning.

Violet would not trust in the back of the cart her treasured plants—the root of lilac, the japonica seedling, the lily-of-the-valley pips, her yellow tea rose. She had heard stories of people going off to live wilderness lives in the great country that had one edge on the Atlantic and reached no one knew how far. And she had been fearful until Amos read to her from the Bible that the wilderness would blossom like the rose; then she had felt less fearful. But Violet had her own feeling about the Bible words. Though she could not read them for herself she knew that there must be a willingness in the heart of man to work with them. So she saw to it that she had with her a bit of loveliness that she might help in the blossoming of their wilderness.

She held the box of plants on her lap, looking down at them often during the journey and seeing instead of leafless twigs and raddled roots the fragrant flowering of lilacs around their door yard. In her ears she could hear the busy droning of bees in a widely blooming bush of japonica. But it was the slender sprouting of the lily-of-the-valley pips that gave her most pleasure in her mind. Loveliest of any blossoming thing to her was that green stalk with its white bells. White was the most beautiful color she knew. Yet when she would say that to Amos he would remind her that the brown of the earth from which the flowers came was a good color too.

Celyndia, sitting on the seat between Amos and Violet, clasped tightly her one sure treasure—the doll Amos had made her from corn husks. The face was a piece of leather on which he had painted small features. The face that Celyndia looked into was a replica of her own and because the lips smiled she smiled too as she looked down at it. Then she hugged her dusky baby closer to herself.  She had wanted a sawdust dollie with a white china face and pretty pink cheeks, but she loved this one because Amos had made it for her.  She held it tenderly and crooned to it, hushing it into slumber.

Amos let the reins lie loose over Cyclops' back. The old horse had a long way to go and the load was heavy.  Amos would not urge him to more than a walk and on the hills he and Violet would get out and walk beside the cart.  Amos looked straight ahead of him, along the horse's back, his vision narrowed to the road between the horse's pointed ears.  He knew that it was a big step he was taking, this move to a new part of the land, far from the familiar, the known, the safe and secure.  Yet he was going far too from the memory of toil as another's chattel, from indignity and privation and the long slow years of servitude. He no longer had his youth, nor the stout strength of his early manhood, but he still had his vision; a compound of words read by a little Quaker girl in a clear voice, words that had burned themselves into his mind and burned away the shackles hate had put to his lips: "Unto

him that loved us, . . . and hath made us Kings
and priests unto God." In his memory he knew
he had been born a king, but it was the little Roxanna reading from the Bible who had shown him
the only way that he could become a king. So
he had lived his life thereafter and so he would
continue to live it as long as strength and manhood lasted within him.

On the morning of the fifth day they came
up the hill to Jaffrey. At the top Cyclops came
to a stop of his own accord, as if he had known
they had come to the end of their journey. Amos
said nothing for he wanted Violet and Celyndia
to speak first.

"What's that?" Celyndia asked, pointing ahead
to the mountain that seemed to lie like a great
wall across their path.

"It looks like the long, long hill to heaven
we've all got to climb before we die," Violet said
quietly.

"They call it Monadnock Mountain," Amos
answered, " 'Beautiful for situation, the joy of
the whole earth—' "

While Amos and Violet kept their gaze on the

mountain Celyndia looked around her. Her eyes took in the frame Meeting House and the row of dwellings near it. She saw that one road wandered down the hill again and that there were other roads leading to houses and farms. She heard voices coming from some of the near houses and she could see blue smoke curling from the chimneys. The thought of other people cooking their dinners made her feel hungry.

"I want my dinner," she said dolefully. "Where is the big folks' house where we're going to live?"

Violet put her arm around the little girl. "We aren't going to live in any big folks' house any more, child. Don't you remember? I told you Amos was going to build us a house of our own."

"Where?"

"Over yonder," Amos replied, "some place where we can get a piece of land with a flow of water through it."

Celyndia sighed. "It's going to be a long time before we have anything to eat then."

Amos reached into the back of the wagon and brought out the box of food they had been partaking of ever since they had left Woburn. The bread was stale and the cheese was hard, but he divided what remained. Then he went to the watering trough and filled two leather buckets, one for them and one for Cyclops. They ate their meal quietly and soon after Celyndia put her head in her mother's lap and went to sleep.

Amos looked over his shoulder at the sun. Past noon now and they were at the end of their pilgrimage. But it would not be the end, he reminded himself, until he had a shelter for his family, not only for this night but for all the nights to come. As he looked around him he thought that there must be a piece of land that such as he could buy in this smiling township under the shadow of the near mountain, a place where he might stake a claim to honest work. Amos got down from the cart. In a soft voice so he would not wake the child he told Violet that he would be back soon.

The arrival of the Negro family at the common had not gone unnoticed. The constable, having his dinner in one of the houses that faced the common, saw them and decided to keep an eye on them. He had thought they were merely giving the horse a rest before going on their way to some settlement. But when an hour later they were still there he decided to investigate. A cart piled high with the miscellanea of housekeeping could mean only one thing for a township and he thought it best to do his duty and give the usual warning. He started across the common at the time that Amos was leaving his family and they met a short distance from the cart.

Amos bowed respectfully as he had long ago been taught to do in the presence of any white man but neither years, suffering, nor hard work could bow the proud carriage of his head. The constable acknowledged the greeting though he could have wished that, being a short man himself, he had not had to look up to the Negro. Before Amos had time to ask if there was a piece of land he could buy for his work and his home the constable spoke up.

"I'm only doing my duty, when I tell you you'd best be gone from this town."

Amos smiled. He knew the formality of the

warning and the reason for it. "Mr. Constable," he said, "I'm looking for a tanner and I'll be on my way soon enough if you'll give me the name of a good one hereabouts."

The constable glanced at him shrewdly. "Got some hides in that cart of yours along with everything else?"

Amos grinned. "Horse hide, maybe."

The constable thought for a moment. "There isn't a tanner nearer than Keene and he isn't what you'd call a good one."

"Then it might be a fine thing for this town if a tanner settled here," Amos suggested.

"It might be a fine thing for the tanner," the constable responded, then he looked at the Negro more sharply—the leather breeches the man was wearing might have been worn by gentry and he carried a pouch that was a pretty piece of tooling. However, no matter what the man's trade, the constable knew his duty would be undone if he did not endeavor to send him away.

"I'm telling you once and for all that we don't want you here, whatever your business," the constable said. "Now, get on your way, all of you.

The next town in the direction you're going is Marlborough." He didn't care what the family of blacks did, whether they stayed or went. He had done his duty to them and by warning them off he had freed the town of any liability for their support should they ever become impoverished.

Amos put his hands to his head in a deferential gesture. "Thank you kindly, Mr. Constable, but I've a mind to make my home here."

"How old are you?"

"Seventy-one."

"How long in this country?"

"I came when I was fifteen."

"How long free?"

"The last twelve years."

"Let me see your papers of manumission."

Amos took from his leather pouch the precious document that bore Ichabod Richardson's name and that given him by Mrs. Richardson, then the marriage paper that had meant freedom for Violet and her child. The constable looked at them all carefully and handed them back.

"This is a rugged country in which to start anew at your age."

"I'm young in freedom," Amos replied, "and I've got my strength still."

"There are eleven other free Negroes in this town and hereabouts," the constable said, "so you won't be without your own kind." He looked at Amos questioningly. "Are you a church-going man?"

Amos smiled. "I've gone to Sunday meeting almost since I came to this country and it was from the Bible that I learned to read."

The faint lines of a smile played over the constable's face. It might be a good thing for the town if the man did stay in it. However, it was not for him to say and not for him to suggest a welcome.

"You'd best go see Parson Ainsworth, that house over yonder," he pointed. "He'll know of a piece of land for you if any one does. He's parson on probation this year," the constable explained. "But we like him so well that we'll be ordaining him in another year."

Amos Fortune crossed the common and knocked on the door of the minister's house. There he found the welcome the constable dared not evidence. Ainsworth was soon ready to discuss the possibilities of a tannery and a suitable piece of land for it. But first he sent one of the neighboring children to the cart with a jug of fresh milk and some new-baked gingerbread.

"Seems like the Lord's doing, your coming here, Amos Fortune," he said. "For we've had too long a journey to make with our hides in years past. Now, you'll want a piece of land with some water on it and not too far from the center."

"I won't need much land, sir," Amos replied, "an acre will do for the start and the brook needn't be much just so long as it doesn't go dry. But I will need trees of fair size and age for the tanbark."

Suddenly Ainsworth slapped his thigh with his one good arm. "I've a piece of my own land for you. It's down the hill toward the mountain, lying west of the common. It's rough and uncleared, but there's a free flowing brook and you'll be within easy reach of all who want you."

"I'd be pleased to look at it with you," Amos answered, and without another word the two men went off down the hill to view the land.

Violet, from the cart, watched them go. After she could see them no longer, she looked down at Celyndia playing in the grass with the little boy who had brought the milk and gingerbread.

"Why is your face so dirty?" the little boy was asking.

"Because we've been far traveling," Celyndia answered.

"Don't you let any one scrub it off," the boy said, "and someday I'm going far traveling too so I can have a face like yours."

An hour later when Violet saw the two men come up over the brow of the hill she knew by their smiling faces that whatever had been decided upon was pleasing to them both. The minister went toward his house and Amos returned to the cart, lifting Celyndia up to the seat before he got in himself. As they drove down over the hill to the rough land by the tumbling brook, Amos told them what had taken place between himself and Parson Ainsworth.

"He won't sell the land to me," Amos said, "but he wants me to use it as long as I like. I'll do so and gladly, and I'll make him a handsome pair of breeches and shoes for all his children."

"He looks a young man to have a many children," Violet commented.

"He's not married yet, but when he is and when they come along I'll make them shoes."

"I've never known you to lack work, Amos Fortune, and here you're making some up beforehand."

"A man has to show his thanks in the way that comes best to his hand," Amos said, smiling to himself.

After they reached the piece of land where Parson Ainsworth had driven a stake into the ground to mark it as on loan to Amos Fortune, Violet unpacked the cart and Amos cut down trees to prepare a rough shelter for the night. But long before evening was upon them, a group of men headed by the parson himself came down the road, followed by a team of oxen drawing a load of boards. The Fortune family and the friendly neighbors worked together and by nightfall there was a shelter for living and the beginning of a fireplace where Violet could cook their meals.

Celyndia slept in a bed that night for the little cot Amos had made for her was the only one they could bring in the cart from Woburn. Amos and Violet slept under the stars while peepers chimed in a marsh nearby and late birds called to each other. They were free. They were starting life anew. They were being helped to get going and the people in the land to which they had come were showing gladness at their arrival.

"God give me strength for many years to do my work well," Amos prayed in the quiet of his heart.

Pin for smoothing

Unhairing knife

Beam

Vat hook

Tanning Tools

Fleshing knife

Spud, for stripping tanbark

# HARD WORK
# FILLS THE IRON KETTLE
# 1781-1789

❧ THAT FIRST SUMMER in Jaffrey
was a busy one. Amos and Violet worked hard
together and Celyndia did what she could, for
though they had been helped with a shelter it
was still far from being a home. Amos went
early to the woods where trees had been felled
and with his barking mallet and peeling iron he
stripped the bark he needed from the great pros-
trate trunks. When he brought the slabs of bark
home it was Celyndia's task to stack them in piles

near the shelter where they might dry in the sun that was gaining heat and strength as the days moved on. Then, when the bark was sufficiently dry, Violet would grind it to a coarse powder in a small mill Amos had constructed so they would have on hand always a good supply of tannin.

The hours of Violet's days were so filled with helping Amos that she had little time to give to her loom. Amos had erected it for her and it took up a good part of the space in the single room of their cabin. Violet, passing it during the day, would stroke it lovingly, thinking of the comfort and beauty its fruits would someday bring to their small abode.

When Celyndia had finished the tasks assigned her, she would run gleefully up the hill to the common to play with the children of the town. As the season advanced, bringing each in its own time a harvest of wild berries, the children would troop off with baskets and pails in search of strawberries, raspberries, blueberries, blackberries. It was still hard for Celyndia to feel that she could rightly go wherever the other children went. But Amos assured her over and over again that the world was hers to walk through, to look at and rejoice in, though he was quick to remind her that the good things were not for any one person to have but for all to share together.

"Look, look, Papa Amos, at my pretty jewels," Celyndia cried joyously when she brought home her first small basket of bright red strawberries.

Amos admired them and Violet saw in them zest for their evening meal, but Celyndia's eyes filled with tears at the thought of eating them. Only Amos' quiet assurance that there would be more for her to find tomorrow enabled the little girl to part with her riches.

So Celyndia enjoyed the eating of the strawberries as she had their picking and her eyes were bright for the next day's treasure.

In the brook that flowed through the woods back of their cabin Amos built a washing place for the hides and skins. When a hide was brought to him, he let it soak in the stone basin for three or four days. Then he drew it out and turned it over to Violet who scraped it carefully. The hair that came off, Violet would save to spin and weave into bed coverings, but the scraping was a slow process and she would have to go over the hide long and carefully to remove all the dirt and impurities.

Near the washing basin Amos dug a pit which he kept filled with a solution of lime and water and into which the hides and skins went after the scraping. There they remained for two or three weeks. Every day the water was drawn out and fresh water let in. Sometimes Amos thought longingly of the better equipment he had had in Woburn. There he had sweated the hide in a smokehouse and the heat loosened the hair easily and made the skin itself more pliable. But he did not long to be back there. He had an acre of land on which he might do the work of his hand, a family to care for, and freedom like the light of day around him. He felt he knew what was good and he had no wish to diminish present good by thinking too often of past days when work was done more easily though no better.

"Amos, there's no lime in the bag," Violet announced one morning.

"Then we must make some," Amos replied.

In the copper kettle he had brought with him

from Woburn he boiled down a solution of ground-up wood, roots and leaves of the trees from which his tanbark was taken. Of this there was plenty in the forest, for though oak bark was best for tanning, bark of hemlock, spruce and larch could be employed, while even the bark of alder and sumach had useful properties. In all his long years as a tanner, Amos was never more glad than he was during the first months in Jaffrey that so much of what he needed for his trade was at hand and could be obtained with no expenditure save that of his own time and muscle.

The last piece of work he had to do before his tannery was complete was to construct a rough yard for the drying of the pelts. Once that was done he was ready to seek business. But he did not have to look far for work had been waiting for him. By mid-summer the people of Jaffrey with hides to be tanned were following the road that led down from the common to the clearing. There, under the shadow of tall trees, within earshot of a running brook, they did their business with the man whose skill commanded their respect.

All during the first year in Jaffrey there was scarcely room in the cabin for anything but the tanning operations. However, by the second year when people came to call for their leather and paid Amos Fortune in cash or kind, his stock of supplies increased and he added another room to the cabin and more comfort to their living. The iron kettle that stood half-hidden in the ashes of the hearth and held the Fortune savings began to be musical with the coins that were collecting in it. Amos did not know how long it would be before the contents of the kettle would be sufficient for him to buy his own piece of land. His soul might long for heaven but his heart longed for cleared fields and a wider brook. A barn with a good sized stall for Cyclops and stanchions for a cow or two. A house with pretty things in it for Violet and Celyndia. And a plot of earth near the house where Violet's flowers might grow freely. He said little about his dream but he nourished it in his heart as the best place for a dream to grow.

People who came to deliver their hides would

often linger to talk with the tanner. Old Amos he was called, yet not so much for age as in affection. A curious smile would light his face when he talked about his work or listened to others tell of theirs. And people went away from the tannery thinking enviously of how happy the blacks were. But only Violet knew that Amos lived by a dream within him though she did not know the dream. Always she thought of him as climbing some mountain in his mind, like that great one to the west on which his eyes would dwell so often and from which he seemed to derive something that was even more than strength.

"Monadnock says it will be good weather today," Amos would announce on a morning when the mountain stood clear against the sky.

"Monadnock says we'd best not leave any leather out for there'll be storm before night," he would say when a veil of cloud like the thinnest gauze capped the mountain's crest.

He knew its moods and he talked to it as a friend, and the mountain never failed him.

"That's a long name—Mo-nad-nock," Celyndia

said one day. "What does it mean, Papa Amos, or is it just big-sounding the way Celyndia is pretty-sounding?"

"It's got a big meaning, Lyndia love," Amos told her, "for they say in the Indian language it means 'the Mountain that stands alone.' "

"Oh," Celyndia dropped her voice reverently. But ever after that when she looked at the mountain she felt friendlier with it; for, child as she was, she knew what it was like to stand alone.

A young man came cantering up to the cabin with a packet strapped to his saddle. "I've come the miles from Peterborough to find you, Amos Fortune," he said, "and I want to know if I can have my hide into leather by the new year. It's as fine a cow hide as you've ever seen and I want it tanned for breeches to wear at my wedding."

Amos looked at the hide, fingering it knowingly. "You can have it as soon as its ready, but I'll not hurry leather. It's had one life. It will take time to give it another."

"I've heard there's a tanner in Keene. I'll take it to him and tell him I want it by the new year," the young man threatened, though he knew that Amos Fortune was the best tanner within miles and he had no desire to take his fine hide elsewhere.

"Take it to him," Amos said, "or leave it with me and you shall have it when the leather is ready." He smiled slyly, "Would you be wanting it any sooner?"

The young man left the hide and rode away and Amos went to work on it. He soaked it well, then he spread it on his beam. This was a wooden horse of convex form, one end of which rested on the floor and the other supported by two legs came up to the tanner's waist. With the hide in position, Amos worked over it with his two-handed scraper. The concave curve of the knife's edge fitted the convex surface of the beam and with slow pushing strokes he half shaved away, half scraped off the hair and epidermis.

That done, he turned the hide over and took his two-edged fleshing knife, cleaning from the inner side all particles of animal tissue and trimming off portions of the skin that would not respond to tanning. Then Violet took the hide and put it through the next process, soaking it for forty-eight hours in sulphuric acid to distend the pores and render it more susceptible to the action of tanning.

Amos had a succession of pits from six to eight feet deep filled with solutions of tannin. Into this ooze the hide went when it was ready and there it would stay for from three months to a year depending on its weight. Every month the ooze was renewed and strengthened, and every day Amos worked in it wearing heavy wooden shoes that were impervious to the tannin. With long-handled hooks he moved the hides and skins up and down, took them out, drained them, looked them over carefully to see how they were getting on, then put them back again. When he was satisfied that the soaking was complete, he would haul the hides out and hang them up to dry.

Many of the coarser hides could be beaten until smooth with a steel instrument, but those requiring special care were passed between wooden rollers. The hide from Peterborough was such a one and Amos Fortune passed it back and forth between the rollers until it was soft and pliant.

The work was done in good time for the young man's wedding day and Amos was glad to have it finished for him and before the cold weather came. During the winter months it was hard to work on big pieces, for the cold and freezing in the pits and Amos saved that time for work on lighter skins and kips that never went into the pits at all but were tawed with alum and salt with the yolk of an egg added if they were to be finished white.

Amos' working week began at sunrise on Monday morning and continued until sunset every day through Saturday. One whole day he kept free—Sunday, and that was sacred to churchgoing and to family life. Work and all its signs and reminders were set as far aside as possible on that day while his thought and his time were given elsewhere. He put off the leather breeches that he wore daily and put on velvet ones with silver buckles at his knees and on his shoes. The striped vest he had worn for his wedding was donned for the Lord's day. He brushed his fur hat and set it on his hair that was now as white as the first snows on Monadnock. In the winter he wore a fur coat and in the summer a deep blue straight bodied coat. Then with Violet in her quiet best and Celyndia in as pretty a frock as any little girl in Jaffrey, they would walk up the hill to the Meeting House.

A special pew was reserved for the blacks in the gallery and up the narrow stairs they would go to it. Amos smiled broadly and Violet bowed demurely as they met others of their race with whom they shared the pew. Pompey Blackman, a friend of Amos' since the Woburn days, who had served five years in the Revolutionary War and come back with his own freedom and a fund of stories to tell, was always there. Sometimes Caesar Freeman or Fortune Little would be present, having ridden over from Dublin. But it was the Burdoo family that took up most of the pew, shivering with cold in the winter, pale with hunger in the summer. The little ones were always more ready to cling to Amos than to their father. And their mother, Lois, turned longingly to words about heaven for she had wearied of finding any peace on earth.

With eager interest they listened to the fine

young preacher, Laban Ainsworth, who had been
ordained minister in the winter of 1782. Impos-
ing and fiery, challenging and inspired, his words
on a Sunday were as forceful as his life on a week-
day. For though his right arm was useless, he
was able to handle a team of oxen, hew down a
tree or plant a field. His words carried meaning
and his congregation was the richer for hearing
them. Amos liked to listen, but he liked equally
well the time after Meeting when people gathered
outdoors bowing to each other, shaking hands and
exchanging news fitting for the Sabbath.

It was a good life he was leading, Amos thought
as he took stock of it from time to time, and
though it was a hard working life it was not
without its joys. The greatest of these came on
a day some eight years after his arrival in Jaffrey
when he became a member of the church he had
attended so faithfully. Amos cherished certain
papers always and among them was that of dismis-
sion from his church in Woburn and recommen-
dation by them for his membership elsewhere.
He had shown the paper to Deacon Spofford and
Parson Ainsworth during his first year in Jaffrey,

but it was not until May 21, 1789, when the church met for the transaction of routine business, that it was voted to receive Amos Fortune into communion.

"What a pity he isn't white," one of the elders commented as Amos left the Meeting House. "He could do so much for the church."

Amos did not hear, nor would he have cared if he had. He knew what the church had done for him and he was glad that membership at last would forge him into closer union. With a smile on his face, he was soon astride Cyclops with Violet riding pillion behind him and Celyndia's thin legs straddling the saddle before him. He wanted to share his good news with some of his own people. Down the Squantum Village road they journeyed and though the season was well advanced into spring, the wind had an edge to it as it came across the newly sown fields. Amos thought with pleasure of the warmth awaiting them in the Burdoo cabin.

Five years had passed since Moses Burdoo, the blacksmith, had died and Lois was having an ever harder struggle in bringing up her brood of children. Amos went to see her often, hoping that some of the good of his own life might spill over into hers that was hedged round by poverty and misfortune. Violet had small liking and less sympathy for Lois. She scorned Lois' inability to care for her family and to rise above the conditions of her life. But she always accompanied Amos on his visits though she kept her silence.

The Burdoo family were singing when the Fortune family arrived. The mournful sound drifted through the closed door out to the road. Amos put his finger on his lips as he and Violet walked quietly up to the door and Celyndia tiptoed behind them. He pushed the door open and they stood on the threshold unobserved. The Burdoos were all in a group by the hearth. Lois sat with the youngest on her lap and the other children gathered around her—Polly and Moses, Philip and Sally. For the length of the song, the visitors standing on the threshold made no move.

> "Swing low, sweet chariot,
> Comin' for to carry me home,
> Swing low, sweet chariot,
> Comin' for to carry me home.

I looked over Jordan an' what did I see,
Comin' for to carry me home,
A band of angels comin' after me,
Comin' for to carry me home.

If you get there before I do,
Comin' for to carry me home,
Tell all my friends I'm comin' there too,
Comin' for to carry me home.

Swing low, sweet chariot,
Comin' for to carry me home,
Swing low, sweet chariot,
Comin' for to carry me home,"

the wistful voices around the fire sang. But when it came to the last chorus Amos nudged Violet and Celyndia and they joined in. The Burdoo family turned around and stared, though they never ceased singing. When the song came to its end, the children flew across the room to bring the visitors to the fireside.

"Uncle Amos, will you tell us a story?"

"A story, Uncle Amos, please, oh please," they begged in their high shrill voices.

"Yes, I'll tell you a story," he agreed quietly, "about that song you've been singing, about Africa."

"About Africa!" they chippered, their voices

sounding like a bevy of birds, for Africa was in a way none of them could explain linked up with heaven and they thought of the two places with the same reverence and ultimate longing.

Sitting on a low stool by the fire with the Burdoo children and Celyndia as close to him as they could be, he told them a story. The firelight in his face made it shine so that Violet's eyes filled with tears at the goodness that was hers. And Lois' eyes filled with tears for the goodness she was heart-hungry for and felt she would never have.

"One time there was a traveler man, way away in Africa," Amos began. His voice had a lilt in it that encouraged the children to make a humming sound to go along with it. "And he said he heard the natives sitting round their fires singing that song, yes singing that song as they sat around their fires. He asked them about it and they told him that another tribe living near the Great Falls had a custom that when their chief was about to die—yes, about to die that old man that had served them well—they placed him in his own canoe—"

Amos paused for a moment but the undertone of humming went on.

"They sat him up straight with all his trappings to mark his rank and all the food he would need for his journey. Then they set the canoe afloat in midstream—yes, in the mid stream of the river they set it floating, far, far from the shore. And they headed it for the falls and the white column of mist that rises always from them. Then the tribe on shore sang the song you've been singing as a farewell to their chief. They could not weep, for he was going the way all men must go—yes, the very way. And they must send him on with strength and not sadness, and so they sang, though their hearts were full of longing. For their chief was a good man and they loved him.

"When the canoe drew near the brink of the falls—yes, the very brink of the falls from which the column of mist was ever rising, they saw their chief stand up in it. Tall and straight he stood and his arms reached upward. As he stood there, a chariot came down out of the mist and bore him up high. Yes, bore him heavenward, further than they could see but to the place their hearts were hungering after and where they knew they would meet him in time to come."

Amos Fortune's low voice came to a stop, but there was a breathless wonder in the faces looking into his. Amos reached out and took Polly's right hand in his left. He took hold of Philip's left hand with his right. Then all the other hands linked together and a circle was formed. Amos began to sing—

> "Deep river, deep river, Lawd,
> Deep river, Lawd,
> I want to cross over in a calm time."

They knew the song so they joined in together with him.

Without words they hummed the song through again, then they dropped hands and looked expectantly at Amos.

He said to them quietly, "Why'nt you all go out and see who can hear the first whip-poor-will?"

Because there was something in his words that made the children want to follow them, they raced to the door, their bare feet thudding as quietly on the floor as on the sandy soil outside.

Lois had her head in her hands and was sobbing softly to herself. Violet took the youngest up in her arms and held the child tenderly while Amos spoke to Lois.

"Things going hard with you, Lois?"

She nodded her head. "Harder and harder as the years go by. When Moses was here it was cruel enough, but now he's gone its even crueller. Nothing to eat, nothing to buy food with, helped out by the town until they're tired of helping me—" she sighed wearily. "Soon the children will be taken from me. Poll will be the first to go, then they'll all be gone. I've not got the strength to go on living, Amos," she said.

Amos talked to her soothingly for a while and when he was ready to leave he told her to send Moses and Philip over to him for they could help in the tannery and he would pay them a penny a day.

Her eyes brightened as if the coins had flashed in the firelight.

"Poll will be cared for," Amos said, "and so will you."

After he had gone Lois Burdoo felt comforted, though she could not say from whence or how since nothing in her life had changed.

That night Violet heard Amos counting the coins in the iron kettle, unfolding the paper notes. She guessed what he was going to do and she knew what she was going to do. Never in her life before had she questioned what Amos did, but he had given her freedom when he had made her his wife and she was determined to use her freedom now. She said nothing that night, pretending she was asleep when he got in bed beside her under the coverlet she had spun and woven.

"You asleep, Violet?" he asked.

His voice was so kind that she could hardly bear the deception she must practise to feign sleep. She made no move—fearful to breathe, fearful almost not to breathe.

She heard his familiar prayer, ending with "Good-night, Lord," then she heard his even breathing long before she was asleep. But she did not weaken in her resolve.

The next morning when he was in the ooze of the pit she took the iron kettle from the ashes of the hearth and buried it in the woods, marking the spot well but marking it so that only she would know it.

# AMOS ON THE MOUNTAIN

◆ EVER SINCE HE HAD established himself in Jaffrey, Amos Fortune had longed to own a piece of land that he could call his. For some time now he had eyed with delight a plot in the east section of the town owned by William Turner, twenty five acres of which Turner was willing to part with for a reasonable sum. During the past year Amos had ridden over more than once to survey the lay of the land—the brook large enough to allow him to excavate basins for his tanning operations; the cleared fields where he could cultivate enough for their frugal needs, and the woodland from which he could get his tanbark and cord wood for the winter. So pleased was he on his last visit that he felt ready to offer William Turner the sum of money that would make the place his. But after the evening with Lois Burdoo Amos had begun to think differently.

He told Violet how he felt as they sat outside the cabin after their noon day meal and Celyndia played nearby.

"It makes a hurt in my heart to see Lois so badly, sadly off since Moses died, and all those little children with hardly a roof over their heads or so much as a crust to eat," he said, his eyes on the mountain but his hand resting on Violet's hands that were folded in her lap.

"What are you fixing in your mind to do for that no-account family?" Violet asked warily, her idea of the Burdoos being far from his.

"Buy a little house in the village for them," he said slowly. "Lois can do a piece of work now and then and the children too. We'll get them some new clothes and help them to a start in life."

"How come you can do such a high and mighty thing?"

"There's pounds, shillings and pence in the iron kettle.  There's enough to help the Burdoos, enough for us to buy a farm—"

"Enough to do both?"

He shook his head.  "No, not at the same time. But I've got a good trade and I've still got my strength.  We'll soon have money again to buy our land."

"Amos, Amos—" she began imploringly, then she stopped.  Once it was his hard-earned money that had been used to buy her freedom.  How could she speak against his doing something with what was his for another in need?

Violet closed her eyes to keep back the tears that had gathered in them, and she felt the pressure of his hand removed from hers as he got up and went inside the cabin.  With her heart straining like a wild thing in a snare and the words she could not utter choking within her, she listened to him as he poked in the ashes of the hearth for the kettle that had been his bank.  She had to hold on to herself to keep from flying to him and telling him what she had done. She was afraid, now, that she had done wrong. And yet last night when it had come so clearly to her what to do she had neither doubted nor been afraid. She would hold to what she had felt then, she told herself. And to what she had done this morning when she buried the kettle in the woods; she would hold as long as her courage held.

Amos was standing in the doorway. She knew it though her eyes were still closed.

"Celyndia—" the voice so kind had an edge to it and the little girl looked up quickly from her play.

"Yes, Papa Amos?"

"You been playing in the ashes with Amos' big kettle?"

Before she could answer Violet spoke. "No, Amos. Celyndia never goes near that kettle."

Amos stood before Violet. "Then you know about my kettle?"

Violet hung her head. It was no good trying to pretend. "Yes," she mumbled.

Amos sat down beside her. He said nothing for a moment, then he called to the little girl.

"Celyndia, you run up to Parson Ainsworth and tell him I've a piece of leather that would be fine for a Bible binding. I'll save it for him if he has a mind."

"Yes, Papa Amos." Celyndia dropped her toys and fleet-footed it from the cabin. She always liked to run errands, especially those that took her to the doors of the big folks' houses.

"Why do you send the child away?" Violet asked.

Amos' voice was low and tense. "We may have things to say that won't sound pretty in a child's ears. Come, Violet, tell me what you have done with my iron kettle."

She opened her eyes and she kept them on the mountain while she told him, speaking her words straight and true. "Amos, I've buried that kettle in the woods and I'll go to my grave knowing where it is before I'll see you giving what's in it to a no-account woman who like as not will be no better off a year hence."

"Violet," he said, and his voice was hard and stern, "you dared to touch my money. You had no right—"

"You gave me my freedom, Amos, and I'm bound to use it once before I die."

"But what made you do such a thing? You're a good woman, Violet, and what you've done is stealing."

Violet cringed. The memory of beatings in her former days as a slave swept over her. But something was giving her strength and she felt she could stand a beating even at Amos' hands if she could be sure that what she had done was right.

"How many times, Amos Fortune, have you been standing on the way to laying hold of your own good life and how many times have you set it all aside? Three times. There was Lily, then there was Lydia, and then you put your all on me. I'm not wanting Lois Burdoo to live in hardship but I'm thinking you've got a right to live in dignity."

"But Violet—" he began.

While the words were strong within her she knew she must speak them. "With all the help the town gave her she never made herself any better," Violet insisted. "The children are getting older.  They're the ones to help her and help themselves too.  You'll do more for them all by giving work to the boys than by giving money to Lois."

"But Violet—"

She would not listen to him until she had had her say.  "There's a fire that burns fast the more fuel goes on it and that's shiftlessness," Violet said stoutly.  "Lois is a shiftless woman and money is just so much fuel to her fire."

"But Violet," he reasoned with her, "we've got good trade.  The money comes in all the time and in another few years we'll be able to buy some land."

"A man has just so many years to live and he should have something that his heart is set on before he dies.  The Lord's been mighty good to you, Amos, and I think He wants you to be good to yourself.  Maybe that's why He let you buy me."

They talked until Celyndia got back from the Ainsworths.  But Amos could not by intimidation, persuasion or reasoning get Violet to reveal the whereabouts of the iron kettle. All that afternoon he hunted for it, but he could find it nowhere. And Violet would say nothing except that she would bring it back to him when he was ready to go to William Turner with it.

Amos tried to drown his feelings the next day when he stamped in the ooze of the pit. He tried to drive them out as he beat on his hides. But it was no use. He could not free his mind of the thought of Lois Burdoo, hungry and without hope, with her little children clamoring for all she could not give them. He wanted to help her in the only way he thought she could be helped. He wanted to do it his way and he could not see that Violet's notion of letting the children earn some money could be of any present benefit.

He found it hard to talk to Violet when he came in for his noonday meal and Celyndia sitting across from them at table looked from one to the other wondering what had come between them. For Amos' face was tense and unsmiling and Violet's eyes had tears in them. Violet felt that she would soon weaken and return the kettle to Amos for the ache that was in her at his displeasure. And yet why was she his wife, she asked herself, but to help him to a good life?

"One more day," she prayed, "let me hold out one more day, Lord, and then You tell me if I've done a wrong thing and should undo it."

And Amos prayed, standing in the ooze, "Give me a sign, Lord, give me a sign, and help me to see it as coming from You. Then I'll know what to do. I'll know it sure as my name is Amos."

That night Amos went up on the mountain, feeling he could no longer abide the sadness in Violet's face and the questioning in Celyndia's. The walls of the cabin had seemed to close in upon him so that he felt he must soon push them aside with the strength of his arms or be stifled. He took a portion of a loaf of bread and a bottle of water for he knew that he would not come back until he had his sign. Violet watched him go and she thought to herself: if, by tomorrow, he still feels as he does I'll know I'm the one that's done wrong. And I'll give him back his own and ask forgiveness with it.

Amos climbed as long as the daylight lasted, across the rocky pastures at the base of the mountain, up the path winding steeply through a belt of woodland. By the time light had gone with the sun and came only from the moon, he had reached the wilderness of rocks and rugged trees that was Monadnock's summit. Once there, he looked down at the land below him, bathed in a milky haze of moonlight. He was breathing heavily and it took him a long time to gain not only his breath but his composure.

Looking from the height made him look back over his own life. He saw, with a sudden start of realization, that just as he had come a far way up the mountain to gain its crest, so had he traveled a far way through the years to gain the point at which he stood. He still had his strength, or a good portion of it. And he had his trade. But that was all. His freedom was assured as well as that of his wife and child. Yet he owned no land, nothing they could call theirs if the chariot came for him soon. He thought about his family and what would happen to them when he was no

longer there to care for them.   Then turning his
gaze toward Squantum he thought of Lois needing help so badly.

Ever since he had had his freedom he had
saved one small fortune and then another.   Now
he wanted to spend once more the hard-earned
savings in the iron kettle and Violet would not
let him.   What right had she to oppose him?   Yet
it was he who had given her freedom.   The word
was meaningless unless in its light each one lived
up to his highest and his best.

"Oh, Lord," Amos said, "You've always got an
answer and You're always ready to give it to the
man who trusts You.   Keep me open-hearted this
night so when it comes I'll know it's You speaking and I'll heed what You have to say."

He found a small cavern in the rocks on the
downward slope where he made a shelter for the
night, and the shelter was welcome for though it
had been warm in the valley the wind blew cold
on the summit.   He thought it would be a night
of vigil, but sleep overcame him and the world
grew silent around him.

What time the great sound came he never

knew, but it was sometime between midnight and dawn when a tired man sleeps his heaviest. When it came he was suddenly as awake as if he had never known what sleep was. Like the bellowing of bulls it sounded as it came over the mountain, like the roaring of the sea. And then it was gone. So held had he been by the sound that he was not aware of the wind that swept over him. But in the faint breaking light of early dawn he saw the bending of bushes near him—the wild azalea and the blueberry laden with blossom, and he knew that a great wind had passed by. Overwhelmed with reverence, he rose and fell to his knees.

The mountain had spoken. He had heard it with his own ears. He had seen with his own eyes nature bow before it.

He remembered hearing Parson Ainsworth and a group of men talking about the Monadnock roar, one day, and they had said that all mountains made such a sound at times, mountains with forests growing up their slopes and summits that lay in the path of storms. The wind blowing along the mountain and meeting another current blowing down the mountain could cause a roar

loud enough to deafen a man save that its dura-
tion was brief. That was what he had heard them
saying in the town. But to Amos on the mountain what he had just heard was the voice of God
and because he had asked to hear it he knew that
he must heed it. He prayed then but it was not
his usual morning prayer. He prayed that he
might understand aright what he had witnessed.

Sitting on a boulder, he broke his bread and
slowly drank his water and watched the light of
day fill up the valley. Mists rose from lakes and
low-lying places putting out white streamers that
the warmth of the sun gradually dispersed. From
stalwart houses standing in wide fields and rugged
cabins in small patches of cleared land trickles of
smoke began appearing as people got life into
their fires. They had their morning meals, then
went forth refreshed and strengthened into fields
and woods to do the work of the day. Watching
the increase of the day and its activities, Amos
Fortune—a man who was landless save for the
kindness of a parson—thought what a good thing
it must be to own a few acres of land. To bring
them to bear. To leave them better than when

they came to one's hand. For land was the wealth of this new country. To have land was to have an iron kettle with money always in it.

Then, up there alone on the mountain, he smiled broadly to himself, for something was dawning in him like the light of morning dawning on the world. He looked up at the wide blue sky arching that much nearer him than when he looked up at it from the valley.

"Thank you kindly, Lord," he said, putting his hand to his head in that small gesture of respect he had long ago learned from the white man. Then he bent over and touched his lips to the ground, but what made him do that or why he did not know.

Violet was working at her loom when he returned to the cabin. She did not hear him enter for the noise she was making with the treadles. She did not know he was there until he stood behind her and put his two hands on her shoulders. She ceased her work and sat silent, not knowing what to say. And yet there was something in the way his hands rested on her that spoke of peace between them.

He said thoughtfully, "Violet, I've come to thinking that the best thing a man can do is to own his own piece of land, for himself and for his family. I'm going to ride over to William Turner's this afternoon, but I'd rather not go empty-handed."

She put her hands to her head and a small joyous sound escaped her. Then she gestured toward the hearth.

Amos turned and saw the iron kettle in its old place, half hidden by ashes.

"Why have you brought it back?" he asked surprised.

When she spoke her words were the first easy ones she had uttered in three days. "Whatever you had a mind to do when you came back from the mountain I wasn't going to keep what was yours from you any longer."

"It belongs to us both," Amos said, "and you were right to guard it."

That afternoon Amos and Violet rode over to William Turner's and signed the deed that put twenty five acres of land, cleared and forest with a brook running through it, in Amos Fortune's name.

And there, by the bank of the brook, Amos built his own house—strong enough to meet the stress of time and the force of storms. He built a barn and a tanyard and excavated basins in the brook for his work. And Violet planted the treasures that she had been tending all the time they lived on Parson Ainsworth's land—her lilac and tea rose, her japonica and the lily-of-the-valley pips.

By the end of 1789, when Amos Fortune was in his eightieth year, he became a land owner in his own right and one of his life's long dreams was fulfilled.

# AUCTIONED FOR FREEDOM

◀▶ WITH THE AID of his neighbors, Amos had built his house before the winter snows came. It was a small house, like many others in the countryside, with a large central chimney and two fireplaces. At first its furnishings were of the simplest. But as the tanning went on and the iron kettle again resounded with the coins collecting in it, Amos added to their way of living things of comfort—feather beds and a writing desk, a chest of drawers and a looking glass, cheese presses and churns, a new wheel for the spinning and a larger loom. Now that he had a barn of his own and cleared fields, he bought another horse so old Cyclops might be turned out to pasture for his remaining days. A cow and a heifer took their places in the barn, and to the tools of the tanning trade were added the equipment of a farmer.

Customers came to Amos Fortune with hides and skins from considerable distances. Men who wanted work well done thought nothing of coming from as far away as Reading and Sterling in Massachusetts, as Amherst and New Ipswich in New Hampshire. The reputation of the Jaffrey tanner had grown steadily. And with a larger place, better equipment and the hire of the Burdoo boys, as well as his apprentice, Simon Peter, who was indentured to him for a period of three years, Amos was able to take on more work. People trusted him not only with skins and hides but in matters of pounds and pence.

One morning Amos opened a letter and read to Violet, " 'Sir: Please to let Mr. Joel Adams have a calf skin if mine isn't out. Let him have one of yours and I will swap or allow you for it. B. Prescott.' "

"Have you a calf skin?" Violet asked.

Amos nodded. "One of the best." And he thought with pleasure of the large barn which enabled him to keep a good stock of leather on hand against just such demands.

There was another letter from Simeon Butters asking Amos to pay Samuel Avery twelve shillings, " 'It being for value received of me,' " Amos read aloud.

Violet asked, "Can you let him have so much, Amos, not knowing when he'll pay you back?"

Amos nodded again. "We owe no one and there are coins in the kettle like a family of rabbits in a burrow." He looked at Violet and smiled the broad smile that meant more than any words. It was a debt of thanks he owed to her and would go on paying as long as he lived. She bowed her head slightly, accepting in silence what she knew in her heart was her due.

Jaffrey had a Social Library and Amos became a member of it. He read its books during the winter when tanning operations were somewhat

in abeyance and discussed them with the citizens
of the town. He was always well informed for
he subscribed to a newspaper. His store of infor-
mation, matched with his ready wit, gave him
opinions that were often sought after. He was
their fellow citizen, Amos Fortune, and more
often than not the prefix "Mr." dignified his
name. He had won his way to equality by work
well done and a life well lived. But his own life
was no guarantee for the lives of those who were
dear to him. Celyndia, now sixteen, had many
friends among the white children. But there
were times when she was made to feel uneasy at
school because of her color and her different ways.
Violet, however, would not let her miss school.
Violet knew what it was to carry through life the
heavy burden of illiteracy and she did not want
Celyndia to bear that along with the burden of
her color. So Celyndia went bravely to school.
But she was happiest when sitting beside the loom
watching Violet weave or sitting at the loom and
weaving herself.

The better things went with Amos, the more
his heart ached for those who received the neces-

sities of life only in the form of charity. The town had again been helping Lois Burdoo with firewood and foodstuffs. But no matter what help she received she never seemed able to rise above her wretched lot. The children went to school in tatters, and even when given new clothes they would appear the next day with them dirty and torn. They could not seem to keep from falling down or tearing themselves on briar bushes.

After years of ineffective help, the town felt that it could not bolster Lois Burdoo any longer. She was given warning that the two oldest children would be put up to Public Vendue on the thirty first day of December. Vendues were auctions at which townspeople could bid for the privilege of affording care to the indigent. The lowest bidder would receive the contract. It was an expedient that pioneer towns had developed to enable them to look after their poor and Jaffrey had been forced to come to it. Many of the people remembered the day in 1774 when at Town Meeting a resolution had been passed: "Voted not to raise money for the poor" and of the human suffering that had followed. For there were always poor, either through misfortune or their own inability to contend with the hard conditions surrounding them. And something had to be done. No town could free itself entirely from responsibility and auctioning off the poor was one of the means by which a township sought to meet its responsibility.

Before the beginning of each new year, notices signed by the town auctioneer were posted in public places advising of the vendue to be held. Celyndia saw one such notice and told her mother of it.

That night Violet said to Amos, "So Lois has agreed to it at last. She's putting the two oldest up to vendue."

"Not Polly!" Amos exclaimed.

"Yes, Polly and Moses."

"But Polly isn't strong enough to work as hard as she'll have to if she's vendued."

"That doesn't matter to Lois. She can't feed the children and the town can't let them starve."

Amos would not believe what Violet had told him until he went to the village late on that raw

December day.  Then he saw the notice posted outside the Meeting House.

There were the names of the town poor, eight in all.  Some of them he knew slightly, but none so well as the two Burdoo children.  Under the list of names he read,

> The above will be put to the lowest bidder who shall board and nurse them in sickness and health and pay every expense for them except doctor's bills which the town will pay, and clothing which the town will provide.  The contract shall continue one year from the first day of January, 1793, when those persons who shall keep them shall remove them to the place which shall next be provided for them if within the town of Jaffrey.

Amos shook his head slowly.  He had not been able to keep away from slave auctions all the years he was waiting for the arrival of a young girl from Africa.  Here was an auction which nothing could keep him from since the fate of a young girl he knew well was at stake.

It was a cruel cold day, that last day of the year, when Amos made his way to the Meeting House where the Vendue was being held.  The wind was blowing hard and he pulled his great coat around him, tucking his chin down into the collar. There was nothing to see, for snow was on the wind and a blizzard obscured the mountain. But still it was there, Amos thought to himself. He turned toward it as he came over the crest of the hill. Stalwart and deeply grounded it was there, though winds raged around it and snow battered against it. The knowledge of its presence gave back to him some of the strength that the wind had taken from him in his walk against it up the long hill.

Entering the Meeting House he slipped quietly into a seat at the rear, hoping to be unobserved. But all who were gathered there knew someone had entered for the gust of cold wind that came through the door. Amos looked over the heads of the people at the eight luckless ones, the poor of the year who were to be despatched, sitting fearful and silent in a group near the auctioneer.

It was a strange kind of auction, this Vendue, for there was no talk and only a little whispering among the townspeople who were present. Some of them looked shame-faced, knowing they were out to get labor in the cheapest way. Others boldly intended bidding on elderly people so they might make a few pounds off the town. All were surprised to see the tanner enter. Amos Fortune's reputation for fair dealing was such that none could think of him as taking part in a vendue.

Lois Burdoo sat in a corner huddled into her thin garments, sobbing pitifully. When Amos saw where she was, he moved over and sat beside her, stroking her hands for comfort and assurance.

The auctioneer started to address the small gathering of people, calling out his wares as if he had so much live stock at his disposal. The first to be auctioned was the fourteen year old Negro girl.

"She may be thin," he said, "but she won't cost you much to keep if she eats little. She's got a good pair of arms and those legs should carry her as far as anyone here is likely to go. What am I bid?" His eyes ranged over the crowd hopefully.

Alexander Milliken of the tavern on the slope of the mountain bid £4.

Lois Burdoo shuddered. "No, no," she murmured, "not a tavern."

Amos whispered into her ear, "It's the last bid that matters, not the first."

There were other bids, but none went lower than two pounds, ten shillings. People nodded their heads as if in agreement, for who could keep a girl in food for a year for less than that? In spite of what the auctioneer had said about the stoutness of her limbs, it was clear to see that little work would be got from a girl as thin as a child with a dazed look in her eyes and a racking cough.

"Going," the auctioneer called out, "going—"

"One pound sixteen," Amos Fortune spoke up in the voice that was clear and strong and known to so many.

The auctioneer gasped. A ripple of amazement ran through the group of people in the Meeting House.

"You must like your town to want to save it so much money," the auctioneer commented. "Going, going," he said, then in a loud voice, "gone to Mr. Amos Fortune. Polly Burdoo, one year, at £1, 16s."

Polly left the huddled cluster of the poor and ran over to her mother and Amos, turning from one to the other, still too frightened to smile at the good fortune that had come to her.

None of the others went so cheap. John Briant got the care of the Widow Combs at £5, 18s. Joseph Wilder got the Widow Cutter at £10, 16s. But the Widow Cutter was lame and so old that it would be nothing but the chimney corner for her. Twelve year old Moses Burdoo was struck off to Joseph Stewart, the first and only bidder, from that day until he was twenty-one, at £15, 15s; half to be paid at the end of one year, and if he live the other half to be paid at the end of the second year. Joseph Stewart knew the boy and had gotten work from him. He was a hard man, but the boy was like a colt and could profit by a firm hand.

"Likely his back will be sore with the beatings he'll be getting," Lois said.

"And perhaps they will do something to his soul," Amos reminded her, for he knew the boy too. "Wings can't grow without a little suffering."

Violet might have small sympathy for the shiftless Lois, but she readily took Polly to her heart, outfitting her in Celyndia's clothes and teaching her some of the duties about the house. Celyndia and Polly were near the same age and Celyndia embraced her new sister warmly. But beyond the flight of a smile across Polly's dark face and a few words, she seemed bowed forever by her lot.

When she sat dreaming by the fire Amos would sometimes call to her to break her from too long reverie and she would shake her head and blink her eyes with a start.

"Yes, Uncle Amos," she would say, eager to do his bidding.

But even if he asked her she could not say where her thoughts had been the while she had been dreaming.

Polly tried to be a help to Violet in the work of the house, but dusting cloth or broom had a way of falling from her hands. Violet would come upon her standing still and staring before her, the task she had been given to do still undone. Polly was eager to work at the loom and Celyndia spent hours showing her its simple mysteries. But as soon as Polly endeavored to do the work herself her hands would slide off the shuttle, her feet would loose their hold on the treadles and her eyes would stare before her.

"What do you think about all the time?" Celyndia asked.

But Polly could never say.

Violet, in exasperation at a simple task undone, exclaimed to Amos, "It's only your kindness that keeps her, Amos Fortune, for anyone else would have returned her to the town long ago."

He smiled in answer. What he had done had been done with good reason and he was satisfied.

Polly liked going to school with Celyndia, but after a few days she brought back a note saying there was nothing the school could do for her since she would not learn.

That evening Amos, with a piece of leather large enough for a jerkin and fine enough for a gentleman, went to see the school teacher. He offered the leather as his gift and begged leniency for Polly.

"She hasn't long with us and what she gets from you will help her where she's going," Amos said.

Because the tall old man with his keen eyes and

fine carriage could not be gainsaid, the teacher
agreed to keep Polly. He wondered, as he
watched the tanner go on his way, who would
have the girl another year, and he thought she
would nowhere find the kindness that she had in
the Fortune home.

Soon Polly could not raise herself from her bed,
but the weaker she grew the more she smiled as
if a kind of content were coming over her being.
Celyndia spent hours reading to her, talking with
her. Violet brought her things to eat. Amos sat
beside her through the long quiet evenings. Polly
asked him for stories and he told them to her, but
more than all the others she asked for the story
of the chariot. After he had told it they would
sing together, her voice following his even though
she could only whisper the words.

Violet sitting across the room at the loom and
Celyndia with the spindle in her hand would
join in.

One night early in November Polly asked Amos
to help her sit up. He put his arms around her
and held her up. She was so light that he felt if
he held a flower on its stalk it could be no heavier.

She held out her hands, resting her right hand in Violet's that were worn and coarse with the care she had given to others, and her left hand in Celyndia's that were supple and strong. Her eyes she kept on Amos. Peace dwelt in her face, a smile hovered over her lips, and for the first time she seemed to be seeing clearly those who were close to her. Her gaze that had always been so far away had come near at last. A small shudder passed over her body. She sat up very straight for a moment, even without the aid of Amos' arms; then she fell back into his arms.

Celyndia started to sob softly. Amos put back his head and Violet saw him shape with his lips the familiar words, "Thank you, Lord."

Violet turned to him with a question in her eyes.

Amos answered it. "I wanted her to die free. I knew she didn't have long when I bid on her, but she's had almost a year of freedom."

"She wasn't ever a slave," Violet reminded him. "She was born free."

He shook his head. "She wasn't free when she was so poor. She's gone ahead now vith a smile on her face and a light in her eyes. Frightened little girl that she was, she's left that far behind and she's crossing Jordan unafraid." His face was glowing, almost as if he were sharing some of the radiance he knew had reached out to encircle Polly.

Violet looked at him. Never before had she felt so much love for this man who seemed to live to give freedom to others. "You'd set all the world free if you could, wouldn't you, Amos?"

He shook his head. "Just the part of it that I can touch. That's all any man can do." He drew the coverlet over Polly's face and reached across the bed to touch Celyndia's hands. "Don't you cry, Lyndia love, you go out and give the creatures in the barn an armful of hay. Tell them what's happened in the house and see if the barn is shut tight, for the wind is blowing cold."

Glad to have something to do, Celyndia left the room. Amos went to the fire to put on more wood, then turning around he spoke quietly to Violet.

"Once, long years ago, I thought I could set a canoe-load of my people free by breaking the bands at my wrists and killing the white man who held the weapon. I had the strength in my hands to do such a deed and I had the fire within, but I didn't do it."

"What held you back?"

Amos shook his head. "My hand was restrained and I'm glad that it was, for the years between have shown me that it does a man no good to be free until he knows how to live, how to walk in step with God."

"But Amos," Violet exclaimed, "look at the people to whom you've given freedom! Lily and Lydia, Celyndia and me, and now you've set Polly free to die happy."

"And go on living," he reminded her gently.

"How is it you're thinking of these things tonight?" she asked him. "Never before have you told me about that canoe-load of your people."

"I used to see Africa in Polly's eyes," he said, "the past and its sorrows and all that was behind, but I've not seen what was ahead for us until just now. Perhaps I saw that in her eyes, too. It's good, Violet. It will be worth the waiting for."

The next day Josiah Carey dug a grave for Polly Burdoo in the churchyard near the lot that Amos Fortune had reserved for himself. A few months later at Town Meeting it was voted to pay Amos Fortune the one pound sixteen shillings in full for keeping Polly Burdoo, even though he had not had her all the year. Amos would not use the money for their own needs. Instead, he put it away in a separate place, saying to Violet that he had a mind to do something particular with it and when he knew what it was he would tell her.

# EVERGREEN YEARS 1794-1801

◘ THE YEARS WENT ON in a quiet way. Violet and Celyndia spun and wove, and their linens were as much in demand as Amos' leathers. Often a man coming from a long distance to leave a hide would not go home empty-handed. Seeing the fine linens that were woven in the tanner's house, he would secure one or more to take home to his wife. It was good that the loom could be so useful, for Amos had begun to feel the fullness of his years. An ox hide was more than he could handle alone, and even the daily tramping in the ooze tired him. But he still carried his head high, and there was strength in his arms and light in his eyes.

Another apprentice had been added to the Fortune household, a white boy, young Charlie Toothaker, one of the seven children of Roger and Mary Toothaker in Lunenberg, in nearby Massachusetts. Amos had known the boy's father in the Woburn days for Dr. Toothaker then lived in nearby Billerica and he had always been a good friend to the Negroes. He had tended both Lily and Lydia in their last illnesses and would never accept any payment from Amos. But now this man, whose father and grandfather before him had been doctors, had written the Jaffrey tanner that things had gone hard with him and that he was being warned out of Lunenberg. He wanted to place his children in homes where they would have good care and, what meant more, the influence of good example. So he had asked Amos if he would take Charles during the years of his minority. Amos had been happy to be able to do something for the kind-hearted doctor. Indenture papers were drawn up, witnessed and exchanged, and Charles Toothaker, thirteen years old, became a part of the Fortune family.

"He's a gentleman born and he's got it in him to be a doctor like his father when he's grown," Amos said to Violet. "But to learn a trade is as good a way as any to start in life."

Amos often took the indenture paper from the drawer where he kept his receipts and read it through, wanting to assure himself that he was doing all he had agreed to do for the son of his old friend. He read aloud to himself,

> This indenture witnesseth that Roger Toothaker of Lunenberg in the county of Worcester and commonwealth of Massachusetts, physician, hath put and doth by these presents voluntarily and of his own free will and accord put and bind his son Charles Toothaker an apprentice to Amos Fortune of Jaffrey in the county of Cheshire and state of New Hampshire, tanner, to learn his art, trade or mystery after the manner of an apprentice, to serve him from the day of the date hereof for and during the term of until he shall arrive at the age of twentyone years. During all which term the said apprentice his said master

faithfully shall serve, his secrets keep, his lawful commands gladly everywhere obey. He shall do no damage to his master nor see it to be done by others without letting or giving notice thereof to his said master. He shall not waste his said master's goods nor lend them unlawfully to any. He shall not commit fornication nor contract matrimony within the said term. At cards and dice or any unlawful games he shall not play whereby his said master may have damage with his own goods nor the goods of others. He shall not absent himself day nor night from his master's service without his leave, nor haunt ale houses, taverns, nor play houses, but in all things behave himself as a faithful apprentice ought to do during said term. And the said master shall use the utmost of his endeavors to teach or cause to be taught or instructed the said apprentice in the trade or mystery he now followeth, and procure and provide for him sufficient meat, drink, apparel, lodging and washing, fitting for such an apprentice during the said term and at the end of said to procure and provide for said apprentice and to learn him if he is capable of learning to read, write and cypher fitting for such an apprentice. And for the true performance of all and every the said covenants and agreements either of the said parties bind themselves unto the other by these presents.

In witness whereof they have interchangeably put their hands and seals this eleventh day of

March in the year of our Lord one thousand
seven hundred and ninety three.
Signed sealed and delivered
in presence of us

*Roger Toothaker*
*Charles Toothaker*

*William Turner*
*Jane Turner*

Amos tilted his head toward Violet as he folded
the paper and put it away. "There are things
Charlie would rather do than learn to read and
write and cypher, but we'll make a good tanner
of him first and that will give us a foundation to
build on."

"He'll learn more than tanning when you've
taught him all you know," Violet replied. "He'll
learn what it is to be a free man."

Since the day Amos had begun to live in
freedom, his life had been a series of curious
accomplishments known in their richness and
wonder only to him. Lily, Lydia, Violet,
Celyndia—they stood like milestones along his
way and behind them all was Ath-mun. Amos
held her always in the tender loveliness of her
twelve years, and because of her need to be cared

for and his longing for her to be cherished, he had dedicated himself to helpless folk. It was Ath-mun who had been the fount of freedom to those others, Amos thought, as he reached back into memory for the beloved sister; he had acted for her and so he would account to her when they met together at the Jordan. Evening after evening, as he sat out in front of his house listening to the clack of the loom, listening to the Burdoo boy beating the hides, he thought of his meeting with Ath-mun.

When sunset wove a pattern of color in the west, he would often walk up the small hill that gave him a wide view of his mountain, Monadnock towering splendidly against the ebbing day. Letting his vision hold it he felt happy; for he was still climbing it though his feet had not been on its slopes since he had turned ninety.

It was during the summer of 1801 that Amos Fortune began to feel he was drawing near the end of the road, but there was something more he wanted to do before he left Jaffrey.

"You won't mind waiting, will you, Lord? You know what it is I want to do and You know it's a good thing for Your children, but You haven't yet shown me how to do it."

His mind traveled far back into memory these days and there were times when the past seemed as real as the present. As a good workman, he had won the respect of his townspeople and of many who came to deal with him from miles around; as a member of another race he was given such place as the white people thought he should occupy. No matter how devotedly he loved the church or how faithfully he served it, he could call no pew his own but must sit with his family in the cold north gallery in the place reserved for Negroes. Accepted into communion as he had been, he must still dwell on the fringe though his heart was at the core. A lifetime had accustomed him to such an attitude but it could not keep him from wanting something worthier for his people.

Violet had no place of sure respect and dignity save in the home he had built for her, though people came from far to buy her linens and gave them honored places in their homes. And even Celyndia was not always free from taunting and abuse. Amos felt he could bear affronts himself, but what was the meaning of a man's life if it did not make the way better for those that came after him? His own back bore the scar the lash had made on him as it broke the skin and branded him forever, not as a renegade but as an object upon which the white man might exercise his power.

It was only a year ago, he recalled, that he had taken a hide for delivery to the Tavern. He would not have chosen such a place for delivery had the owner not specified it, and when he got there he would have turned away if he could for the man was not in such a state as one with whom he liked to do business.

Amos Fortune had stood in the doorway and the owner of the hide had called to him from the bar. "What do I owe you?" he had asked.

Amos answered, "Five dollars," proud to be giving his price in the new tender.

"Putting on airs, he is," the man laughed back. "A Pound Sterling is what I'd call it."

Amos stood tall and straight on the threshold facing a room full of men, all strangers to him save Alexander Milliken. "It's your leather but it's my price," he said quietly, "and we've each got a right to our own."

The man guffawed loudly and lunged across the room to seize the leather. Amos was tempted to hold on to it until he received his money, but feeling the man's strength he let the leather go. He was one against a roomful, for Milliken was not the man to take sides against any of his customers.

Amos said, "Five dollars is the price you agreed to when you brought the hide to me."

The man laughed again and tossed a handful of coins on the floor. "Money has lost its value since then. Take what you can get and be glad of it."

Amos was obliged to get down on his knees to pick up the coins that had rolled all over the room.

A fire was burning in him as he trudged home with the pittance in his pocket and no redress at hand. For when a white man chose to be over-ruling there was little the black man could say or do. But Amos would not go home while hate burned within him, so he sat on a boulder by the roadside and faced his mountain.

That was the day the men of Marlborough and Dublin had set fire raging on Monadnock to drive out the wolves and bears that had been doing damage among the herds pastured on the slopes. Amos watched the fire climb slowly at first, starting from a dozen different places; then like a wall of destruction it moved up the steep sides until the flames met and linked in a vast pyramid of fire at the summit, consuming everything that could be consumed and leaving the mountain bare and smoldering.

Hate could do that to a man, Amos thought, consume him and leave him smoldering. But he was a free man, and free at a great cost, and he would not put himself in bondage again. So Amos got up from the boulder and walked home and his friend Moses walked with him, the Moses who had followed a pillar of cloud by day and of fire by night and kept himself free from the bickerings of his people so he could be their leader.

"You're late," said Violet, wondering at his silence.

Amos agreed, then he told her of the fire on the mountain that he had been watching.

"Did you bring back good money for your leather?" Violet asked.

"I was paid for it," Amos answered.

Violet heard him putting the money away in the stone crock. She was surprised that it was going there, for that was a special fund Amos was creating; but she smiled to herself, so many coins must mean he had been paid well.

Amos thought of all this as he sat in front of his house during the long summer twilights or watched the sun go down in glory behind his mountain. Amos told himself that if people knew what it was they did that caused suffering they would no longer do it.

As the days went on and he was aware of strength running from him gently like sap from a fallen tree, he felt heart-hungry for heaven. Sometimes it was like a hurt within him the longing was so intense. For years now he had shared almost everything with Violet, but he could not tell her of the feeling that was growing within him for he could not find the words to ease what for her would be pain. But he went on praying that he might know what it was he could do to help free the white man and bless his own people. Then one day, clear as the signs had always been in his life, he knew what it was.

It was on an October morning when the world stood crisp and clear in its first frostiness that Amos Fortune walked over the familiar road to the town to call on Deacon Spofford. In one hand he carried a stout oak staff and in the other a leather bag into which he had emptied all the money in the stone crock.

"Good morning, Amos, and how are you?" Deacon Spofford was a tall man so they faced each other eye to eye, and though his manner was grave his smile was the evidence of a warm heart.

"Well as I've been for a long while," Amos answered. He paused for a moment, then he went on, "But I'm thinking it's time to make my will."

"Perhaps so," the deacon agreed, "but you're still strong and you've got a fine trade."

Amos shook his head. "I've got a clear notion of what I want to do with my property and I'm thinking when a man has that it's a good time to make a will."

"It is a good time."

"And it's you I want to execute it."

Deacon Spofford looked across the table at the dark face, strong of line and forceful, marked by kindness. He wondered what white man of comparable years had brought such renown to the town as had this tanner who lived so frugally and did his work so well.

"I should be deeply honored, Amos Fortune," the deacon said as he reached his hand across the table to clasp the black man's hand.

Between them they drew up the will. Amos, declaring himself to be weak in body but of sound and perfect mind and memory, said that he wished to leave to Violet, his beloved wife, his household goods, all the improvements he had made on the land and whatever profit there would be from his real estate.

Deacon Spofford nodded. "That's a good farm of yours, Amos, and into it you've put heart as well as muscle. Whether Violet keeps it or sells it, it will care for her all her natural life. And here is my oath, my friend, that while I am alive no one shall take advantage of her."

Amos smiled his pleasure at the deacon's words, then he went on to make provision for Celyndia, his adopted daughter. To her he left the furniture she was using, the loom and foot wheel that she might always have a means of livelihood, and he commended her to Violet's care.

"Have you any wish of your own that you would trust me to carry out?" Deacon Spofford asked.

Amos nodded. "I'd like a handsome gravestone for myself and one for Violet when her time comes," he said quietly, "to be erected in my lot in the graveyard."

"It shall be done," the deacon replied, "and William Farnsworth shall do it, for there's no man living among us now who can handle mallet and chisel better than he. What will you say on your gravestone?"

Amos Fortune was silent for a moment, then he said, "I'd like Parson Ainsworth to write whatever goes on my stone, and on Violet's too."

Deacon Spofford made a notation of all that Amos Fortune had said.

"There's one more request," the soft voice went on, lower than ever since what he had to say was so meaningful to him that he could speak of it only with reverence. It was the answer to the prayer he had been praying all that summer; it was the designation of the fund that had been collecting in the stone crock.

"Two things stand out in my life," Amos Fortune continued, "the way the mountain stands out in this country. Church and school. I've got the money saved and I'd like you to make a handsome present to each." He laid his leather bag on the table and drew out a hundred dollars. "For the church," he said, "to purchase a silver communion service."

"There are things the church has greater need of," Deacon Spofford reminded.

The old man shook his head. He had seen his vision and he must see it through. For that holiest of moments that was shared by all alike, nothing could be too beautiful. And he knew, too, that nothing he could give the church would carry further the whole meaning of his life.

"Let it be done as I say."

Deacon Spofford wrote it down. "So be it," he said. "It shall be done."

Amos unwrapped a handkerchief in which he had put the rest of the money from the stone crock—two hundred and forty-three dollars in all. He counted it out slowly as he laid it on the table before Deacon Spofford. Among it was the money received from the town for the care of Polly Burdoo, and some of the coins were those given him at the Tavern for the leather he had delivered there.

Deacon Spofford noted the amount and wrote after it "for the school." Then, quill poised in hand, he looked across the table at Amos. "And will you say what should be done with it?" he asked.

Amos answered, "The town shall use the money in any way it sees fit to educate its sons and daughters."

"I have heard that those in your care have not always fared well at the school," Deacon Spofford said as if he were asking forgiveness of Amos Fortune.

"That is why I give the money to the school," Amos replied as he rose to leave. There was nothing more to do but sign his name in the presence of three witnesses. This was done as Roger Gillmore, Jacob Baldwin and Oliver Jewett were called in to subscribe their signatures.

Amos Fortune walked slowly home, thinking of the disposition he had made of the last money he would ever earn. Humbly he prayed that as the boys and girls learned more they would know what they did and so do only what was worthy of men and women. He was happy. He felt light of heart and a buoyancy came into his footsteps.

"You can come any time now," he said, looking skyward, "for I'm ready."

．．．．．．

In the churchyard in Jaffrey, New Hampshire are two handsome headstones. The slate has

weathered well and William Farnsworth's chisel-
ing is clearly readable.  They say:

Sacred
to the memory of
Amos  Fortune
who was born free in
Africa a slave in America
he purchased liberty
professed Christianity
lived reputably and
died  hopefully
Nov. 17, 1801
Aet. 91

Sacred
to the memory of
Violate
by sale the slave of
Amos Fortune by
marriage his wife by
her fidelity his friend
and solace she died
his widow
Sept. 13, 1802
Aet. 73

A silver communion service was purchased and
was in use many years and the fund designated
for the school in Jaffrey is still in use.

A facsimile reproduction of Mr. Fortune's signature has been used on the front cover.